MANAGEMENT IN THE PROFESSIONS
guidelines to improved professional performance

BY THE SAME AUTHOR

Survival in Business

MANAGEMENT IN THE PROFESSIONS

guidelines to improved professional performance

by MICHAEL ALLSOPP,
FSVA, FFS, AMBIM, LMRSH

BUSINESS BOOKS

First published 1979

ISBN 0 220 67011 0

Printed in Great Britain by T. J. Press (Padstow) Ltd., Cornwall, and bound by R. Hartnoll Ltd., Bodmin, Cornwall, for the publishers, Business Books Ltd., 24 Highbury Crescent, London N5.

To the memory of my father

C.G. ALLSOPP
Architect

Contents

Preface

In recent years the increasing number of books and magazines devoted to management and its techniques has been a reflection of both the growing complexity and difficulty of business life. The demand for such information also indicates the determination of management and managers to succeed. There are few areas of activity that have seen such refreshingly frank disclosure and discussion of the problems encountered, errors made and techniques evolved. The professions have lagged behind industry in this self-appraisal and attempted improvement in performance.

Many professional people do not really wish to know or hear about ways of improving efficiency or management techniques. Their strong sense of independence renders advice from others, particularly those outside their own discipline, unwanted. Some have remained aloof and somewhat defensive whenever their practices or charges have been discussed. The time is long overdue when they should ventilate their thinking with management philosophy. The enlightened public of today, not to mention the businessman confronted with ever-increasing pressures on his profit margins, is only interested in receiving demonstrated service, excellence and value from professionals. It is not interested in tradition for its own sake, restrictive practices, entrenchment or vested interests in economic privilege.

Caution is necessary when considering management in the professions, in particular when comparing their performance and progress with industry and commerce, to recognise their particular circumstances. While there are many instances where the attitudes of management techniques of industry can be of great benefit, care must be taken to ensure that they are used in such a way that there is no diminution of ethical standards or public confidence.

However, many professions, particularly the more established, are approaching the problems of the future with attitudes firmly rooted in the past. Others, some more newly formed, seem primarily concerned with recognition, the enhancement of their dignity and even the creation of a protected status. Since the governing bodies of the professions are democratically elected from a generally conservative group of people, they will naturally tend to be conservative. Most councils take pains to ensure that they reflect the geographical distribution of their membership, and others take care to ensure that different grades of membership are represented. Nevertheless there is a well-developed predisposition among most councils towards preservation of the *status quo*. This is not a tendency peculiar to the professions but to institutions in general, and is as much a characteristic of the group as self-preservation is of the individual. History demonstrates this but reminds us both of the great danger to the institution that reform will come from without if it fails to come from within, and of the dangers of government by a minority because of the apathy of the majority.

The selection of professional goals is therefore a matter of importance. Professional knowledge, while correctly forming the bedrock, is often identified as the sole objective when, in reality, it is only the means to an end. There is a marked difference between the academic and theoretical and the creative and practical, and these aspects are not always given their proper balance in training the professional. The profit motive and commerce generally are often regarded with disdain, and the client gets the service that has always been given rather than the one he needs, particularly where low levels of competition inhibit the development of new services. This book examines some of the ways in which changed attitudes and the adoption of management techniques might enable professionals to utilise their resources more efficiently and to achieve or improve upon their ideal of public service. When all is said and done, it is often the task of the professional to make complicated things simple and not simple things complicated.

In recent years some professions have been the subject of public and press criticism on a scale far too great to be ignored. Official inquiries, although somewhat narrowly directed towards restrictive practices, have also found that the public good has not been served to the extent claimed. The defensive posture adopted and the evidence put forward by many of the professional bodies have served more to increase than to allay the misgivings of many observers.

The professions are undoubtedly concerned to ensure that standards are maintained and mindful of the hard-won status that they have achieved. In some cases they have developed from conditions of unruly and unfair competition, and there is a fear that any relaxation of disciplinary control may threaten their livelihood and injure the public interest. The extent to which these dangers are real or imagined cannot be determined, though it is noteworthy that where restrictive practices have been relaxed, there appears to have been no reduction in standards. A sense of responsibility and a need for the esteem of one's professional colleagues are powerful deterrents against the lowering of standards. But is this not a sterile debate? Are these the *real* issues of importance? It is very doubtful. The interdependence between the professions and the public can only be constructively based on mutual trust. This in turn can only be based on demonstrated performance, not upon protection.

If it is accepted that the future strength of a profession depends largely on its value to the public, then efficiency in the application of professional knowledge must rank alongside the possession of that knowledge. Thus the subject of management, in the handling of clients' affairs and in the internal conduct of practice, will assume a growing importance in education and professional thinking.

'This is a practice
As full of labour as a wise man's art.'

Shakespeare

CHAPTER 1

Management and the professions — an introduction

All professional people are involved to varying degrees in management, and their effectiveness, indeed their success, may be determined as much by their skill in that sphere as in their discipline. Demand for management ability may arise in a number of ways:

1 In the conduct of their own affairs, particularly if they are in practice on their own account or in partnership.
2 In the attainment of their clients' objectives, which may require a wide variety of management skills. Professional assignments involve the application of knowledge and this requires planning, coordination and control.
3 In achieving their employer's objectives. This will occur in private practice and where the professional is employed in industry, government services, teaching or even a charity.

The function of management

There is no universally accepted definition of management, perhaps because of the comparative youth of the subject and also because of the great diversity of the activity. The word 'definition' itself implies an exactness which could be an unwelcome constraint upon so free and formative a concept. However, there is an accepted consensus and little difficulty arises.

For the purpose of this study I have adopted the following definition:

> 'The selection of goals and the planning, procurement, organisation, coordination and control of the necessary resources for their achievement. Management is concerned with the dynamics of circumstance and activity and is generally motivated by the need to economise in the use of resources and time in achieving predetermined objectives. In commerce, management is concerned with efficiency in the conversion of opportunity and resources into wealth.'

It can be seen that management is largely preoccupied with the future, and the manager must spend a great deal of his time mentally ahead of events. To the manager the past is a valuable experience and the present is a test of the competence of past planning, but it is the future that is the real and continuing challenge. The future can only exist in the mind, and the activities of forecasting and selecting goals are objective and abstract intellectual exercises that require assimilated experience and imagination. The inadequate can only rely on guesswork or 'hunch' and manage by instinct.

Objectives and profitability

It is important in all activity to have an accurate and sound idea of one's purpose, for without clarity of purpose misdirection of effort is probable. In commerce and industry it is normally profit or, to be more accurate, profitability — that is to say, the achievement of the maximum return on the capital employed in order to increase the wealth of the proprietors, and to compete effectively for the further capital necessary for growth.

Sometimes these fundamental aims are obscured by an unhealthy attitude to profit or an excessive preoccupation with the technical aspects of the business itself. Examples of the consequences of such confusion of purpose have been all too numerous in recent years. Without adequate profits, which partly spring from healthy attitudes towards them, the confidence of investors cannot be retained, surpluses for reinvestment will not be available, and employment opportunities will diminish as business stagnates. It is equally important that society as a whole should maintain a healthy respect for profitability and those who achieve it.

In the professions, which generally escape the searchlight of financial commentary normally directed upon the public company, profitability is often a private matter for discussion by the partners behind closed doors. In such conditions practitioners can all too easily find that their true objectives are obscured by a preoccupation with procedure and detail. One is then reminded of the comment of Sir Henry Maine: 'So great is the ascendancy of the law of actions in the infancy of the courts of justice, that substantive law has at first the look of being gradually secreted in the interstices of procedure.' (*Early Law and Customs*, page 389). It is because of this inherent human tendency that it is important for the professional to maintain a clear understanding of personal goals and an overview of the *real* needs of the client and the present and future role of the profession in relation to society.

The foregoing reasons would in themselves provide ample grounds for emphasising the importance of carefully selected objectives, but there are more. Capital resources and revenue are usually limited. For this reason the selection of the optimum objectives in terms of service and profitability is critical and in fact among the most important decisions made in the business world.

Planning

For all these reasons we will return in more detail in Chapters 2 and 3 to the work of the professional in policy formulation, forecasting, the evaluation of various courses of action, planning and decision-making. From the day the specialist embarks upon the final stages of his professional education, he is continually being called upon to advise upon the relative merits of different available courses of action. His ultimate standing may largely depend upon his decision-making ability, both within his discipline and in affairs of management.

Most work undertaken by the specialist is complicated, and its smooth execution usually requires planning ability of a high order if the goals are to be achieved. Planning, sometimes of long range, is also necessary in dealing with an individual's career, taxation, and the development of a private practice. Routine matters are not exempt, for planning is necessary for the dispatch of many smaller assignments. An almost total absence of any systematic programming and progressing of work in some solicitors' offices is doubtless a principal cause of delays so often encountered in that profession and not infrequently commented upon by the courts and media.

Organisation and delegation

The design of an organisation to achieve predetermined objectives is, for many, almost as important as the work itself. For example the architect or engineer responsible for any large undertaking must master the technique of organisation in uniting and coordinating the different and sometimes conflicting disciplines in his team. Failure to achieve satisfactory standards of project management, be it the flotation of a public company or the design of a structure, will damage the individual's reputation, no matter how skilful his professional work.

As a professional practice grows in size an increasing proportion of the equity partners' income may be derived from the profits of the firm rather than their individual work. Thus the professional may slowly shift from total reliance on his personal skill to a position in which he may be more concerned with the procurement and management of a flow of work. In this more administrative role the selection of personnel, the organisation of the business and the control of quality may be matters of greater preoccupation than the detail of the professional work itself.

Some may find this loss of direct involvement a heavy price to pay for the growth that comes from success. In other cases it may cause difficulty for not every man who is successful as a professional proves to be a good organiser, especially if he has not trained himself for his new role. The growth rate and ultimate size of a firm is probably influenced as much by the proprietor's ability to develop management skill as it is by his ambition. Outside their practice many professional people assume considerable management responsibilities for organising their clients' affairs or at least for advising to an extent that will be heavily relied upon.

When the subject of organisation is examined in more detail, one sees that it is not merely an attempt to find the best way of 'getting things done', but is, in fact, a deeply influential matter. The character, style, outlook and satisfaction of people within an organisation depends to a considerable extent on its structure. An ill-conceived organisation cannot be given a dynamic character by exhortation.

The subject of organisation naturally leads to that of delegation, one of the essential arts of business. Many professional assignments can only be discharged by teams; they are far beyond the scope of an individual. The acts of delegating and designing the job of the person to whom work is transferred affects morale and efficiency. This theme will be returned to in Chapter 3.

Coordination, control and review

Managers have been defined as people who make things happen. No matter how well conceived a project may be, or how detailed the planning, control is essential to ensure that results are not distorted by shifts in circumstance or inadequate performance during execution. The manager is concerned to ensure that the task in hand achieves its predetermined results within the time and cost allowed. Control is made possible by monitoring those aspects that will indicate departure from plan or budget in time to allow remedial action. Each task undertaken also contains a lesson. If skills are to be improved and experience is not to be forgotten, a process of review of work undertaken is essential and of great importance in training staff for increased responsibility. Both control and review are discussed in Chapter 4.

Personnel recruitment, selection and administration

Whereas the medical profession utilises costly equipment and others may increasingly rely on computers, the professions are generally labour-intensive rather than capital-intensive. Thus the reputation and prosperity of a professional firm is principally based upon its people. It follows that recruitment and selection are matters of the greatest importance and that the quality of the firm will largely be the sum of the quality of its principals and staff. For this reason the process of recruitment and selection of staff will be reviewed in Chapter 5, for failure in this area will greatly reduce both the capability and potential of the entire unit.

The ability to recruit and select personnel of the right quality and drive is not in itself enough to assure success. The administration of personnel must be of a high standard if their continuing contribution is to be assured. In many cases the honeymoon period with new staff is brief, and routine reduces the relationship to one in which the parties tend to take each other for granted. In this situation both parties lose.

Communication

The invention of the telephone, telex and data transmission has accelerated communication, but the end result often remains poor because of the failure of the human element. How often one hears the comment in crisis, 'If only I had known sooner' or, 'I wouldn't have done that if I'd known the facts'. The hallmark of the good manager is that he communicates effectively. Nor is communication confined to correspondence and telephone calls. Much information is transmitted in meetings and their conduct will be dealt with under this heading.

The professional as a manager

The starting point for all who aspire to management is the attainment of a good standard of self-management. Clarity of personal objectives, planning of one's individual career, selection of the most suitable employer, the ability to plan and organise one's own work, satisfactory control of the affairs in hand, good communication with clients, colleagues and partners all add to professional potency. On some occasions personal efficiency makes a more valuable contribution to progress than loyalty or length of service. For these reasons the work of the professional as manager will be analysed in Chapter 8.

Financial management

Some professions are closely associated with business, and in the case of the accountant, for example, good financial management may be expected. However, there are many callings that are remote from financial affairs where the practitioner may be at risk through ignorance. Sound financial management is essential, not only for success, but for peace of mind within a practice.

In addition the demand for skill goes further because advice given may touch upon a client's financial affairs. For a professional person to proceed with a bland disregard for his client's financial considerations can undermine his advice. These aspects are therefore examined in Chapter 9.

Buying professional services

The professional not infrequently selects others to contribute to a team. Thus the architect selects quantity surveyors, the solicitor chooses counsel, the doctor recommends consultants. In this capacity the professional places his client wholly or partly in the hands of another, the client usually being unable to make a judgement for himself. In this buying role the general practitioner risks his own reputation.

It is equally important in the marketing and selling of services to see oneself through the clients' eyes and to appreciate fully their point of view. Failure to achieve this empathy can cause remoteness or, worse, arrogance.

Marketing and selling

Many professionals may shudder at the thought that the words marketing and selling can be used in relation to the services. Such a reaction is an evasion of reality. Not only must a flow of work be realised, but the right type of work must be brought in if the firm is to gain strength. Whether the process is overt or covert, it is essential for survival, no matter how restricted the actual activity may be by the rules of conduct that constrain the individual or practice.

Marketing and selling are not confined to the more commercial activities. Those professionals engaged in government service must be aware of the process if they are successfully to project the assistance available to those in need. It has often been found, particularly among the elderly or infirm, that aid has been shunned because of a misguided pride or sense of independence, which can only be overcome by an 'educating' process involving marketing and selling techniques.

Thus marketing and the way in which commercial organisations undertake this work will be reviewed, along with the way in which these established techniques and attitudes may assist the practitioner.

The responsibilities of management

The sole practitioner with a small number of employees will be obliged to handle all aspects of management in his own practice. Apart from the never-ending increase in the volume of paperwork that afflicts people in business, he or she must achieve a grasp of all the aspects already touched upon in order to create maximum effectiveness. It is not an easy situation and is one in which a conscious effort not to expand is probably necessary if the individual's main satisfaction comes from the vocational aspect of his work. In some cases, for example that of a barrister, the administrative burden may largely be carried by a managing clerk, and the increasing volume of work encouraged by success can be limited by raising the fees charged (though this can have the opposite effect).

In the larger firm the problems may be extensive, especially in the assembly and control of specialist or multi-disciplined teams. In these cases some specialisation among the partners will be necessary in dealing with management affairs in a similar manner to the allocation of work between directors of a company. Also the administrative function may be of such a magnitude that full-time managers, not qualified in the profession in question, could be necessary. For the multinational firm, probably servicing the needs of multinational clients, the management challenge may be of the highest order and involve the recruitment of locally qualified people for branch offices and adroit international financing. Thus the range and magnitude of demand for management skill is wide.

Similarly the size of one's commercial clients and the tasks they generate can vary greatly. The extremes are typified by the lone professional advising a single person and the engineer supervising a major civil engineering project on another continent. It is not, therefore, only the sophistication of the work in hand that can determine the level of management skill required, but the scale of the operations undertaken and the size and sophistication of the client. It is for each person to decide, having acquainted himself with the principles of management, on the level of attainment necessary for the work he does.

And what of the responsibilities of management, about which there has been growing awareness in recent years? The narrow concept of making a profit is probably less applicable to most professional people, many of whom have a strong sense of vocation. It is nevertheless worth noting that the narrow profit motive has, to a great extent, been replaced by such concepts as the moral responsibility of people in influence, the protection of the consumer, the preservation of the environment, the need to maintain full employment and the dire challenge to fight inflation. As a rider to the definition of management given at the beginning of this chapter, one may add:

> 'Many of the responsibilities of management arise from the employment of people, the power to condition human needs and desires, the creation of the wealth necessary for the maintenance of the security of the community, the

attainment of its social claims and the preservation of democracy.'

As major contributors to informed public opinion and as providers of essential skills, there is a heavy responsibility on each and every professional person.

Checklist - Chapter 1

MANAGEMENT AND THE PROFESSIONS — AN INTRODUCTION

1 To what extent does the person or firm under consideration rely on management ability for the performance of its work or profitability?
2 Do those concerned appreciate the nature of management and its responsibilities?
3 To what extent does the work in question require planning and an awareness of the future?
4 Are the fundamental aims of the firm and its managers the subject of formal discussion or are they taken for granted or obscure?
5 At what level and with what degree of formality are policies determined?
6 Has the organisation of the firm been designed for the attainment of objectives or has it grown according to demands over the years?
7 Does the firm assume far greater management responsibilities in an advisory capacity when dealing with external affairs of clients than are generated by the demands for internal management of the business?
8 What systems coordinate and control the progress of individual assignments, departments and the firm as a whole?
9 Are the lessons learnt on individual assignments fed back into the management systems so that they benefit the firm as a whole?
10 To what extent is the firm labour-intensive?
11 How is recruitment and personnel selection organised?
12 Does the quality of personnel employed match the demands of the work coming into the firm?
13 What is the labour 'turnover' record and how does it compare with similar firms?
14 Are the managers adequately aware of the

importance of good communication and does the firm maintain a dialogue with its professional association?

15 What is the quality of communication with clients and could it be improved?

16 Are the departmental managers and executives marked for promotion trained for their enlarged responsibilities?

17 Do financial controls vividly and speedily indicate the progress of the firm to the partners?

18 Does the firm procure its financial resources in the most profitable way?

19 Has the firm an accurate idea of the capital really employed by it?

20 Are other consultants retained by the firm selected on the basis of friendship or some formal procedure to ensure high standards and good purchasing on behalf of clients?

21 What rules govern marketing and sales activities by the firm and how does it ensure an adequate supply of suitable work?

22 Is the responsibility for procuring work clearly assigned or left to chance?

23 How are factors of importance that cannot be quantified, such as client satisfaction, measured?

24 What sense of social responsibility is felt at senior and management level and what significant changes are taking place that affect the profession as a whole?

25 Do personnel policies provide for the development of staff, the enrichment of traditional jobs and adequate training?

26 To what extent is the firm regarded as a 'business' or a vehicle for the practice of the discipline?

27 In the event of the unexpected illness or death of a senior partner, would the firm be exposed to risk through lack of direction or control?

'Happy is your grace,
That can translate the stubbornness of fortune,
Into so quiet and so sweet a style.'

As You Like It, **Shakespeare**

CHAPTER 2

The objectives of professional practice

The success of any organisation is greatly influenced by the extent to which its members are motivated by its stated objectives. Each person must be able to relate their role and work to that of the whole team and its goals, and whenever possible to see their personal effort as a contribution. Where the part people play is obscure, the development of their sense of responsibility to the firm as a whole will be inhibited; and where purpose is vague, performance will suffer. An inescapable responsibility of management is to decide upon its aims and to formulate and promulgate a clear plan for their attainment.

This is an area of much weakness in commercial and professional circles. It is common to find companies that have prospered because of the talent, hard work or opportunism of the owners, but are without policy and vulnerable through imbalance or too much reliance on past success. Weakness in this area can extend beyond the individual business to entire industries or professions, usually to be exposed by recession and to result in disillusionment and unemployment. Internally the morale and vitality of a team will be checked if management fails in this duty through lack of effort or imagination.

The limited notion that the primary aim in business is to enlarge profits is both inadequate and dangerous. It is inadequate because modern business and social conditions impose wider demands on all those engaged in any activity involving the public, and dangerous because the criterion of profit alone can too easily sacrifice the future.

The question of business morality now extends from the individual consumer to the international arms deal, and in many areas the adopted compromise is scarcely refined beyond thinly veiled hypocrisy. Codes of practice abound and many are yet to be integrated in common law. Consequently the horizons and responsibilities of those who are engaged in business, enter into contracts, employ or are employed are now greatly extended beyond pure profit in financial terms. Complexity and conflict abound. Enlightened policy-making is inevitably a task to be approached with some humility.

These are not questions for which there are standard answers. The circumstances of every individual, firm, company and even country vary. The aspirations, opportunities and resources of each unit are different. While policies may be similar, each must be tailored to suit the case in question.

Generally speaking the commercial company, particularly if its shares are publicly quoted, will focus its attention on achieving the optimum balance between short- and long-term financial performance. As it competes for finance, its management will be influenced by the motives of the expert investor and the ever-observant financial commentators. The private company can pay more heed to the wishes of those who control it.

The professional firm, especially if it is unincorporated and unlimited in its liability, is an even more private affair. It is not obliged to file its annual accounts and can, if it wishes (and can survive), be run according to the personal whim of the controlling proprietors. Here we are concerned with a more formal approach. What then are the factors that must be considered in the formulation of the sound policy? They are numerous and sometimes conflicting, and the order of priority will vary in each case.

1 The development of the firm as a whole.
2 The needs of the individual partners.
3 The needs of the staff members and their development.

4 The development of the profession as a whole and its services to society and to the individual clients, upon which the entire structure is built.

The development of the firm as a whole

The goals of a firm as a whole may be conceived in a number of ways, but most commonly in performance achievements leading to financial targets. What is important is that objectives should be determined not only for the company as a whole but also for its component parts.

'Objectives are needed in every area where performance and results directly and vitally affect the survival of the business.'* The organisation with spearhead 'money-making' functions for which well defined strategies exist, but which is drained by objectiveless support functions, is too common.

Financial performance

Financial performance is traditionally thought of in terms of annual profits and sometimes more vaguely and dangerously in terms only of gross fees brought in. The profits generated are undoubtedly a measure, but profitability is a better concept because it embraces the additional idea of the return on the capital invested in the business, i.e. the return to the owners of the equity in the business as well as the reward for the work undertaken.

In the case of capital-intensive industries the importance of return on capital employed is obvious, and though it is easy to think that it is of minor importance in a labour-intensive professional activity, it is wrong to ignore it. Ill-informed critics of professional charges often fail to acknowledge the necessity of providing an adequate return upon money invested in fixed and working capital. The proprietors of a business should have an accurate idea of their investment and the return that would accrue to them from alternative places. The return should reasonably reward them for their use of the

*Peter F. Drucker, *The Practice of Management*, p 52, Mercury Books.

money and the risk taken in providing it. Furthermore recent high inflation has focused attention on the need to make increasing provision for the replacement of costly assets apart from the additional investment necessary to provide more advanced and expensive equipment as technologies progress.

Profits, after taxation, must be sufficient to meet the following demands:

1 A proper level of remuneration for the partners for the work done and their past personal investment in attaining their skill.
2 A return for the risk they take in providing the capital of the firm at a level that will encourage desirable investment in new and improved assets.
3 A provision for increases in working and fixed capital as the firm expands, that is, to sustain increasing debtors, stock and work-in-progress.
4 To provide for increased reserves to fortify the firm against set-backs.

There is little chance of real growth where the proprietors regard their capital as a price to be paid for the benefit of self-employment. The return for risks taken, the encouragement to make further investments and provisions for future expansion are as real as the need to earn money for work done. The financial health of the firms that constitute a profession should be of prime concern to the professional bodies. Where diligent work and good organisation leave firms inadequately financed to meet future demands, then the profession as a whole must be in decline. Where that profession provides an essential service to society, that concern should find expression in Parliament in an atmosphere of constructive political thought.

Certain important financial ratios arise in setting financial goals and monitoring progress:

1 The target income and profit per partner.
2 The income and profit per employee.
3 The ratio of expenditure on 'earning' as opposed to support staff.
4 The target income and profit for each department and the target cost of support functions.
5 The ratio of 'new' business to that generated by existing clients.

6 The ratio of expenses to gross income earned.

It is for each business to consider the best way in which to give financial expression to its several parts, branches, divisions or departments. The way in which targets are expressed is important. Those responsible for a particular function should be able to see, feel and control the factors that condition their performance.

The size of the firm

The optimum size for a firm will vary according to its activity, location and circumstances as well as the management capacity of those who control it. Its rate of growth will be similarly determined by these factors as well as by the desire of its proprietors to expand. The intensity of the commercial motivation of the partners will be a major influence. It is common for senior equity partners to rely increasingly on the profits generated by junior partners and staff. To the extent that this is natural in running a business, and a fair reward for building it, this is right. However, where it is carried to excess it will create difficulties that may lead to conflict between the 'major' and 'minor' partners. Where such a gap forms, the resulting loss of aspirant young partners will both weaken the firm and annoy the clients. Thus the needs of all the partners and staff must be recognised in calculating the firm's financial aims.

Performance objectives

Turning aside from purely financial targets, we find the more commonly visualised performance objectives upon which financial achievement ultimately rests. These are usually seen as standards of performance or professional attainment. Examined from this viewpoint we find goals expressed in the following typical ways:

1 To advance by specialisation. Unless the firm is situated in a large city or in a location of regional importance, a sufficient volume of work may not be available to permit

specialisation. Thus the aims of a business may be expressed in terms of the location, which may extend across national boundaries.

2 To accomplish leadership in a local, regional, national or even the international scene.
3 To achieve professional eminence in practice or research.
4 To use a professional life as a springboard for other activities, e.g. entry into politics.
5 To achieve a quiet and enjoyable life. Some people are built for comfort rather than speed. In a free society there is no compulsion to achieve profit, only an obligation to serve clients with competence.

The needs of the individual partners

While the sole practitioner may tread a lonely path, he is spared the task of combining the aims of individual partners. It is a challenge with an infinite range of solutions from the completely autocratic rule of a dominant partner to the equal voices of a large committee. It is a process as varied as human personality. The interests of individual partners will seldom coincide, and the success of a firm may largely depend on the way in which the partners' ambitions are combined. The realisation of that potential will in turn be conditioned by the relationship between their combined aims, the needs of the clients and those of the staff.

Difficulties illustrate this point more eloquently than successful solutions. For example, the requirements of a senior partner who has accumulated sufficient capital for his needs are in marked contrast to those of the recently qualified and lately married new entrant to the partnership. The situation may demand accommodation if new talent is to be attracted and retained. Similarly, the need for additional working capital to finance expansion may conflict with the pressing personal needs of the partners of a young firm. The distribution of profit between the provider of capital, the manager of it and the employee has always been full of tension and will remain an area in which those with fine judgement can score a major advantage.

It is not only the size and distribution of profit that can generate tension. The attitude towards profit may vary. The firm with little profit consciousness, or worse, a disdain for profit, makes an uncomfortable roost for the ambitious. Regardless of the size and type of firm, the partners may be assumed to rely upon it for their income and probably the growth of their wealth. If the need for healthy profits is not commonly and properly appreciated, priorities will be illogically ordered.

As with financial goals, performance objectives will reflect the wishes of the controlling partners as influenced by their colleagues, though opportunities for specialisation, research work and absence for postgraduate training are normally more easily accommodated than financial adjustments.

Objectives and the influence of change

In reviewing performance objectives so far we have taken the desires of the partners as a starting point. We have also taken for granted that a partnership can choose its professional aims. This is not always the case. As with the industrialist who is excessively orientated to his product and fails through producing what *he* wants, instead of what the market wants, the professional too can err. The scale and level of the error can vary. On a national level it is possible for a profession to continue offering a traditional service for which the public has a reducing need and consequently to be late in developing the services that are required. At the level of an individual practice, it is not unknown for a firm to enter a period of decline because of its failure to respond to changing local demands. For example, industrialisation can change the character of a town; the average age in rural areas may increase as young people seek opportunities in cities, and immigrant communities can transform the character of a district. These external factors may demand a change in the response of commerce and the professions alike if they are to avoid obsolescence. Some professions have much to learn from industry about response to change and the need to modify their attitude to their marketplace and their role.

In reviewing a firm's objectives one must, in addition to grasping the internal factors, understand the external shifts to which it is subject. These may include:

1 Changes in the country's international role and economic strength. This can be of particular importance to multinational practices operating in developing or declining countries.
2 Changes in government as seen in those countries where democracy is waxing or waning. This again is significant to multinational practices or those that serve multinational companies.
3 Changes in international, national or regional prosperity may bring unemployment or a decline in investment in certain industries.
4 Amendments to law can reflect changes in national attitudes to business ethics or standards of conduct and may have impact on those involved in such activities as advertising, brokerage, finance or agency.
5 Advances in law, commercial practices or technology may produce entirely new professions or branches within those already established, for example the development of the computer or management consultancy in the accountancy profession, the growth of television and the decline of the film industry.
6 Changes in taste and fashion can make that which was unacceptable to one generation acceptable or tolerated by a succeeding one, for example the declining congregations in the churches or the practice of abortion.

These shifts, sometimes caused or encouraged by the professions and at other times resisted, resented or completely beyond their control, may necessitate a reaction in order to maintain congruence with society. Sound management demands that those who create policy should have a sharp weather eye on these horizons.

Then there are those internal structural changes which inevitably occur in a firm, for as with the individuals that form it, it cannot remain unaltered as it develops.

Internal changes

1 Changes in the ownership of the equity or shares in the firm caused by death, retirement, expansion, resignation or negotiation. Such alterations can result in fundamental changes in the outlook and management of the whole, particularly if control moves suddenly from one generation to the next or into the hands of another firm by sale or merger.
2 Changes in management where important functions such as personnel selection or the marketing of the firms services are reassigned.
3 Changes in the availability of fixed or working capital caused by alterations in ownership, fluctuations in the economy, capital transfer taxes, increasing or diminishing distribution of profits, losses or personal needs of the partners.
4 Expansion and, to a lesser extent, consolidation can influence the character of a firm as internal relations become more or less personal and communication lines lengthen or shorten in both vertical and horizontal dimensions. Similarly expansion by the addition of new activities can materially alter the feel and outlook of the firm and involve a redefinition of its basic objectives and evolution of a new character.

Review of objectives

It is important to develop a constructive attitude towards change. The professions tend to conservatism and are predictably averse to accepting the new until it has been subjected to the closest scrutiny. Where this process enhances the reliability of their professional judgement, and in doing so benefits their clients, it is well founded. However, where it is an instinctive resistance to change, it can become wholly negative, inhibit progress and foster stagnation. Sometimes it may conceal privilege or self-interest. Reactions to change are best illustrated by taking a few familiar examples.

The negative response

This group is characterised by its resistance to all forms of change. While stability is an admirable characteristic of most professional activity, it is possible by standing rigidly still to be in reality moving backwards in relation to one's environment. Caution can imperceptibly become inertia, conservatism can mask self-interest, tradition can become a refuge and professional etiquette can dull competition. There is always a possibility, if not a probability, that those who are senior members of a profession — if only by age rather than achievement — will inhibit its development by their conservatism. If a reasonable quantity of younger blood is not allowed to flow through the management of a professional firm, it will probably suffer from hardening of the attitudes more quickly than a commercial organisation, for the professions are generally more protected from the rude effects of competition. Such firms contribute little to progress except perhaps to provide ballast at the cost of simultaneously producing drag. In extreme cases they may be right, but often for the wrong reasons as they are entrenched for safety rather than reason.

The weathervane response

This type of response is characterised by ever-changing attitudes, which in turn arise from lack of thought about the firm's role and environment. This type of firm does not resist, encourage or create change because it is barely aware of the world outside. It does not contribute to the body of professional opinion because its members probably drift away from their professional bodies from the day of qualification.

The opportunist or self-centred response

Those who are motivated solely by profit are often attracted to change because they detect short-term opportunities in it. They speculate in, rather than develop, the subject they handle. They are often able to build up relatively large organisations quite quickly, but the resulting business is often dependent upon their personal flair. Sometimes the seeds of ruin are sown in such firms by the weakness of the leader in personnel selection and delegation, which flowers when a reversal in the economy exposes the inherent weakness of the firm's structure and subordinate talent.

This is not to say that such firms do not make a contribution for they are often innovators of great skill. Many an amendment to legislation has been necessary to stop up the loopholes discovered by such talents for the benefit of their clients. Found mainly in the commercial professions, they will argue that their skills are for their clients' benefit and their profit. But one cannot help wondering whether, when they leave or retire, they leave their profession in a stronger or more developed state than when they joined it. There are exceptions that fall both in this and at the same time in the next, more constructive, category.

The response of leadership

Here self-advancement, the progress of the firm and the development of the profession as a whole is found in reasonable balance with the needs of the individual client and society in general. Within the partnership the individual needs of the partners will be understood and the development of the succeeding leaders a natural and continuing process. The firm as a whole, the departments and the individuals will know their goals and be able to gauge their success.

Such an elegant balance is difficult to obtain and requires maturity of judgement to maintain. Inevitably periods of imbalance will occur. In many spheres it is difficult enough to get a constant level of mediocrity. But the chance of success will only arise where the alternatives have been seen, weighed and selected with care. And that is the responsibility of management.

Summary

Clarity of purpose is a prerequisite in the creation of that unity of purpose from which a firm derives momentum and morale. Profit, return on capital or speed of growth are dangerous monitors if taken in isolation, particularly where professional attainments and a sense of vocation contribute much to the satisfaction of the labour. However they cannot be ignored, for long-term stability and the health of the firm must rely largely on the adequacy of the reward for the investment in acquiring the skill and in providing the capital of the firm as well as the risk and work undertaken. Thus financial goals must be balanced with those of performance.

Performance aspirations may determine the size and location of the business, for specialisation may necessitate operation in a large community or at least a regional catchment area. In choosing and ordering priorities regard must be paid to the needs of all the partners and the variations that happen between those of different ages and stages of development.

The constant review of objectives must become part of routine management if external and internal changes are to be anticipated and reconciled. The variations of response to change, from the ultra-conservative to that of true leadership, are infinite. The challenge to management is to attain the right poise rather than a popular pose and to develop long-term strength, not short-term gain. An overview of the profession and the firm as well as society and the client is an essential starting point in the quest for that special formula best suited to the firm in question. Empathy combined with wisdom is more valuable than sympathy combined with good intention.

Checklist – Chapter 2

THE OBJECTIVES OF PROFESSIONAL PRACTICE

1 Does management recognise the importance of clearly defined objectives?
2 Who is involved in formulating objectives and is a fair balance achieved between those concerned?
3 How often are they reviewed and are they written, formally agreed and announced?
4 Are clear objectives understood by all those who contribute to the success of the company?
5 Can they measure their progress towards the attainment of their goals?
6 Do the objectives, expressed in financial terms, properly reward the investment of the partners and provide for their retirement?
7 Will capital transfer and other taxes inhibit or check the growth or prosperity of the firm?
8 Would junior partners or senior staff be able to improve their material positions by transfer to a different firm?
9 Would a combination of junior partners and/or senior staff be in an advantageous position in founding a new firm? That is, is there a threat of defection of a group within the firm?
10 Will the planned growth in the firm be adequate to accommodate the development of partners and key staff in financial terms and also to provide for their enhancement in professional terms?
11 How do local laws in overseas branches affect the development and control of the business, and to what extent is it able to maintain that position in future years?

12 Does the conduct of the firm recognise the tax needs of its proprietors, and how can these needs best be met?
13 Do the partners have adequate opportunities for postgraduate development?
14 At what intervals do financial ratios reveal the progress of the firm?
15 Do department managers and key staff participate in the formulation of policy?
16 Does the firm periodically review its position against that of its competitors and its relationship with its clients?
17 Do the firms' objectives accommodate the needs of succeeding partners and the retirement of those currently in control?
18 Is the firm currently confronted with any problems or difficulties in business or taxation that should be brought to the attention of the professional bodies concerned?
19 Does the practice find its professional body aware, sympathetic and active?
20 Do the partners compare their objectives with those of other firms?

'We work not only to produce but to give value to time.'

Delacroix

'The reward of the General is not a bigger tent, but command.'

O. W. Holmes, Jnr.

CHAPTER 3

Planning and organisation

In deciding upon the overall objectives of the firm the partners will have clarified its operational and financial goals. In the following stages of planning and organising they will be determining the way in which to translate those ambitions into reality. They will know what level of professional reputation they want to gain or maintain, how innovative or conservative their services will be, the volume of work that they wish to undertake and productivity they must achieve, the resources they will need, the profitability they hope for, and their policy for the development of their staff. But much detail will remain to be worked out, and the degree of success will be greatly influenced by the care with which this is done and the vigour and intelligence with which it is put into effect. In this chapter the planning process and the creation of an appropriate organisation to undertake the work of the firm is reviewed.

The attitude with which one approaches planning has a significant effect on its quality. Firms engaged in repetitive work or continually responding to external demands, over which they feel they have no control, sometimes claim that there is little value in the exercise. Others, perhaps more successful, are preoccupied with an increasing volume of work. Because planning is a domestic matter and not immediately productive it is all too easily deferred.

The error in these views lies in a failure to appreciate that the process of converting a broad strategy into tactics necessitates the following exercises, all of which are of great value to any business:

1 It involves a closer scrutiny of the overall objectives and may expose mistaken assumptions.
2 The plan and programme provides a foundation for subsequent measurement of performance, which is essential for proper control.
3 It deepens the understanding of past and existing activities because it requires the analysis of past achievements, statistics, financial ratios and trends.
4 It focuses attention on those factors or resources upon which the firm is dependent and over which it may not have control. This may reveal trading dangers to which it is exposed and highlight the need for contingency plans.
5 It is the first step in generating an awareness of the unity of purpose of the team because it involves participation by all those who manage functions upon which the firm relies. It especially assists the integration of marketing plans into the daily thinking of key personnel who may otherwise misunderstand the contribution that they make.
6 It permits an assessment of the financial implications of the plan, and in particular will reveal the capital required to achieve the goals.
7 It emphasises the need for good communications and exercises the communications system among those who participate in the planning work. Additionally it reminds those concerned of areas of interdependence and the need for teamwork.
8 It produces the information upon which the subsequent design of the organisation will depend.
9 The analysis of detailed objectives or stepping stones in the attainment of the ultimate goals will be set against a time scale, and this emphasises the dynamics of the activities being considered. Plans without a programme are as dangerous as charts without a scale. If managers are to develop into people who really make things happen,

they need to be aware not only of events but of *when* they should happen as well as *why* and *how* they must occur.

The foregoing list of benefits, which is by no means exhaustive, more than adequately demonstrates the folly of the attitude that planning is impossible or a waste of time. Perhaps it further explains why the absence of planning is so often a characteristic of the sleepy or inefficient firm. Just as there are benefits for those who do plan, there are penalties for those who do not; and they are worth brief mention as most professional people nominate specialists in the course of their work upon whose performance they and their clients rely. In fact professional people are purchasers of professional services on a large scale, e.g. solicitors instructing counsel, estate agents instructing solicitors, accountants consulting tax advisers and doctors seeking the opinions of specialists. The weaknesses of which to beware are:

1 Firms that are habitually late in completing work assigned to them or who seem unconcerned by the time taken to complete their work.
2 Firms which are obliged to rush work in order to meet promised delivery dates.
3 Firms that initially underestimate potential difficulties or risks and seek amended instructions.
4 Firms that underestimate costs.
5 Teams that are inadequately staffed or lack resources to provide a good performance.
6 Firms whose staff lack good morale or initiative.

These defects may not in themselves be of a degree that amounts to professional incompetence, but nevertheless they represent poor value for the fees paid.

The planning function

The momentum that drives the planning work along must come from the top and the first question that arises is 'who should do the work?' This will be determined by the size of the firm and subject to the following principles:

1 Ultimate responsibility should be borne by a partner.
2 A working group or committee comprising those

responsible for each area of activity will be necessary to ensure full participation and balance. This should include:

a Each operational department.

b The person responsible for financial planning and control and perhaps accounting.

c The person responsible for administration and support services and personnel management.

d The person responsible for marketing.

e Where research and development achievements in the future will determine the strength of the firm, the person responsible for that activity. In some circumstances the research and development function may have a more important contribution than those reporting on the reactions of existing clients.

The construction of the planning group must match the circumstances. In a small firm it may amount to the meeting of two partners who will share the management functions between them according to aptitude. In a large firm it may take the shape of a series of small-scale weekend conferences resulting in a number of smaller working parties delegated to specialist studies upon which they will report back. What is important is the fact that unless people who are subsequently to be held accountable for performance are contributors to the plan, it may be received with indifference or, worse, cynicism.

The quality of chairmanship and efficiency of the secretarial function are paramount. The person responsible for planning must possess, in addition to the qualities of a good chairman, an objective, forward-looking and constructive attitude and command the respect accorded to those of proven management ability. The natural choice of a senior partner may not be the best one, particularly if he is hard pressed by other responsibilities. In this case it may be more effective to appoint a deputy chairman who can allocate sufficient time to maintain momentum and engage in detail, always providing that he has an adequate overall view of the firm and of the partner's policy in order to achieve balance and accuracy of direction. The planning work should itself be the subject of a programme in order to maintain consistent progress and regular review.

The planning process

Even in the smallest firm it is unlikely that an acceptable plan will be achieved at the first attempt. This is partly because of the complexity of the matter and partly because the necessary organisation cannot be devised until the plan is drafted; this second task will invariably involve adjustments to the plan. The adjustments to accommodate this 'chicken and egg' effect usually involve compromise. The planner may therefore anticipate a series of drafts as ideas are clarified, gain acceptance and improve their fit or are discarded. The process will move through the following stages, the sequence typically being:

1 Translation of the policy into a series of defined and measurable programmed events and financial achievements.
2 Analysis of the activities necessary to achieve those events and their financial implications.
3 Analysis of the resources required in terms of manpower, buildings, plant and capital.
4 Consideration of the organisation and its structure.

The raw material provided will be the policy statement, which may be in the broadest outline terms, and the knowledge of past and existing resources. Both will need refinement and expansion.

The policy statement

This will be the product of the thinking reviewed in Chapter 2 on the objectives of professional practice. It will state the agreed policy of the partners for the future conduct and probably the expansion of the firm over periods of one, three or five years. Of importance at this stage are the operational and financial targets that have been set. These may be expressed as:

1 The expansion or contraction of the number of partners, provision for the partial or total retirement of partners, facilities for the prolonged absence of partners for post-graduate training or sabbaticals.

2 The objectives of the firm as a whole and of each department, coupled with an indication of the priorities to be accorded to each and the time scales for the measurement of progress.
3 The financial targets of each function expressed in terms of target income or profit.
4 The type and volume of new business which it is hoped to attract (see also Marketing, Chapter 10) and any services or specialisations to be commenced or abandoned.
5 The opening or closure of any branch offices.
6 The expansion or relocation of the main office.
7 Any resources to be invested in research or non-commercial activities, e.g. political or local government.
8 Any changes to accommodate new equipment or technology which will alter organisational requirements and staffing needs or increase the range of services offered.

The policy statement, being a strategy for a number of years, will probably not contain the detail of year-by-year activities. The next step is to convert the document into a programme showing the events against a time scale. Having completed this, it will be possible to add the detailed activities and minor events that must precede each major 'stepping stone' in the plan. The draft plan will reveal the following trends and events set against a time scale:

1 Changes in gross fees to be earned.
2 The addition of new staff or opening and closure of departments or branches.
3 The expansion of fixed assets such as buildings or equipment.
4 Changes in the volume of work in hand and working capital requirements.
5 The scale of marketing success needed to sustain the plan.

In short, the programme will produce sufficient detail to reveal basic errors in the policy statement, if any have crept in, and to reveal the resources in terms of finance and manpower that will be needed, together with the rate of demand.

At this point the plan and programme will be sufficiently detailed that one can challenge its feasibility. This challenge starts with the following fundamental question. 'Having regard to the past and present performance of the firm, and having forecast economic trends and external factors such as competition, is the target trend both realistic and reasonable?' It may be that, taking inflation trends into account, the firm hopes to achieve little more than stagnation. More dangerously it might reveal upon comparing future hopes with an extrapolation of past achievement that the plan is too ambitious.

The plan will also now be in sufficient detail to permit critical examination of further important aspects. Too much optimism about the rate of acceptance of new products and services is a common error, particularly by younger firms pioneering novel consumer or client benefits. Caution should be the watchword in such forecasts, and wherever possible commitments should be terminable or short term until early experience provides a more positive basis. Certain regions are notably slow to accept new practitioners, particularly if they are not local people. Unable to advertise, many professions can only anticipate slow rates of growth compared to commercial firms. The planner and those who consider the feasibility of plans must carefully weigh the probabilities of success and the risks inherent in optimistic forecasts.

The analysis of current and past records should reveal accurate ratios for calculating the probable requirements to meet new targets. While it is usually reasonable to assume maintained productivity, assumptions based on increased performance, particularly from staff yet to be recruited, inevitably add greater uncertainty to calculations. As will be seen in the section on organisation, the potential of existing staff as well as the ease of recruiting new staff must be considered. Any delay in recruiting key people may upset calculations. Many regard the acquisition of new clients as the main limitation on growth, but recruitment can be no less formidable a problem, especially in boom periods. The manpower requirements of the plan will therefore require careful consideration both as to feasibility and cost. The latter is essential for the budgets that will be prepared at a later stage, even though the broad financial implications will be continually in everyone's mind throughout the entire planning process.

The establishment's resources in terms of accommodation and equipment must be reviewed. Increases in staff generate demands for increased working space, furniture, equipment, management and welfare facilities. These can represent a high cost, particularly in city locations. Detailed inquiries will be needed into the relative merits of purchasing, hire purchase and leasing, in order to estimate the capital required or additional revenue needed to service these items. Some professions now utilise equipment of great sophistication and high value, which may lead to considerations of cost-effectiveness and the level of utilisation of new aids.

Some of the most valuable information that flows from planning work is that which forms the basis for budgeting. The costs of manpower and other facilities can be expressed at each stage of the plan, and a calculation which will reveal the extent to which the programme is self-financing or will require additional capital can be made. These are matters more fully discussed in Chapter 9.

Organisation

To put a plan into effect without organisation is to invite chaos. Up to this point structure has been ignored. The whole firm and its independent parts have been considered but not their interdependence. Decisions have been made on the way in which the work is to be allocated, the order in which the parts are arranged and the system upon which they will operate. In short, the plan must have life so that the firm will have vitality and function efficiently. Again one must start at the top, which is the source of leadership and motivation and the origin of coordination and control. It is immediately apparent that organisation is a part of planning, and from this it follows that to design an organisation and then to plan work to occupy it profitably is to put the cart before the horse — an error to which a surprisingly large number of human beings seem susceptible.

The theory and practice of organisation is a large subject upon which many leaders have contributed a considerable volume of thought.* Consequently it is a subject where one is working according to general principles and guidelines to achieve the best result in each case, conditioned by circumstances, resources and aims. There is no 'ideal structure'. Some of these themes merit consideration before professional firms are considered in detail.

Specialisation

Most advances in technology and virtually the whole system of modern commerce and production are only possible because of specialisation and delegation. Most complex activities are now beyond both the compass and capacity of the individual. Specialisation has brought about a great enrichment of knowledge, and delegation has increased individual and group capability to an equal extent. The essence of both lies in accomplishing the optimum use of time and manpower. The advantage gained and strength of the assembled skills depend on the logic with which they are arranged, as well as the quality of leadership and motivation of the team. In the professions the boundaries of a specialist's activities are often determined by the curriculum of the discipline. This in turn imposes a responsibility on governing bodies to ensure that training matches existing and future demands. Advancing or changing technology not only creates new specialisations but also necessitates the continual review of demarcation lines to ensure congruity with the needs of society and principles of good organisation. Conservatism motivated by the protection of vested interest can, in the long term, debilitate a profession or trade. Thus the grouping of skills which constitute a speciality is an important preoccupation for those concerned with the vitality of a profession as a whole, as well as the efficiency of an individual firm or professional team.

The subdivision of the total work to be undertaken into specialist jobs which represent the nuclei of related activities is, therefore, partly traditional, partly dictated by training and partly a matter of organisational design. In the professions this

*Pugh, Hickson and Hinings, *Writers on Organisations*, Penguin Modern Management Texts.

is frequently (though not invariably) done on a functional basis. Thus a law firm commonly comprises individuals or departments dealing with conveyancing, litigation, matrimonial affairs, etc; an estate agent customarily divides the firm into functions specialising in domestic sales, commercial sales, valuation, structural surveying, etc. The small firm or sole practitioner that can not subdivide work in this way is unable to offer the same depth of knowledge across the spectrum of its work, though this can be offset by the use of external specialists. Compensation for this weakness may also be found in the more personal service of the small unit and the fact that it escapes the problems of organisation and communication found in larger structures. However, it can now be seen that apart from the basic influence of custom and training, it is the size of the firm that is often the greatest constraint in determining how the work is to be shared among the partners and then delegated.

The nature of the work may not readily permit its allocation by function. In highly private or personal matters it may be found, and often is, that the lay client only wants to deal with one person in whom he has built up confidence. Damaging resentment may occur if the client is directed to different people in a firm according to the nature of the problem. The client who will be directed without demur to the electrical bay or engine shop in a garage may baulk at similar treatment in a hospital or professional office, as those in group medical practice are well aware. In such cases, and where the work demands functional specialists, the work may be controlled by allocation on a client basis and then delegated to functional departments supporting the practitioner in charge, for example, where the general practitioner is supported by specialists at his local hospital or the solicitor seeks the opinion of counsel.

Of paramount importance is the fact that some activities are of such a personal nature that they must sometimes compromise the tenets of organisation theory and practice, and it is quite right that this should be the case. Where circumstances demand this, the client will need the most careful and sympathetic education to accept the change, a fact not always given its due weight by such large-scale operations as the National Health Service. The first level at which to consider specialisation is that of the partners, for confusion here will probably spread throughout. Where two or more people set up in business together they are often, but not always, of complimentary skills, so that the first division of labour is natural. Where they are similarly skilled then it is necessary to analyse and allocate the responsibilities. This may be done in a number of ways:

1 According to skill and experience indicated.
2 By the allocation of clients according to:
    a Type.
    b Size (mainly in commercial cases).
    c Geographical location.
    d Original contact.
    e The clients' express wish.
3 The importance of the client in local affairs or to the firm.

The legal responsibility for the conduct of a client's affairs is that of the partnership, and the personal responsibility of a qualified partner may amount to a requirement.

Apart from the partner's professional responsibilities, he will probably assume certain management roles in order to share in such work as financial planning and control, liaison with professional bodies, marketing and personnel management. The partnership as a whole may make the final decisions in such matters, but detailed work is nearly always necessary and should be allocated. Clarity produces accountability and this in turn usually improves performance. It also avoids the confusion of overlapping and the danger of gaps caused by unallocated responsibility. When the volume of work reaches a point where it is beyond the capacity of the partners themselves, then staff are necessary; these in turn may be grouped or grow into departments and one enters the realms of delegation and organisation structure. The point is also reached where the principals become managers, not just of their own work but of people, and the demands for management skill grow in proportion to the size of their business.

Delegation

The art of delegation is one of the most valuable talents that the manager can cultivate. Furthermore, failure to do so will in all probability not only inhibit progress but actually subtract from it. Delegation is also the key to the preservation of executive sanity.

It is necessary at the outset to differentiate between the role of a person to whom work is delegated and an assistant. True delegation involves the effective transfer of responsibility and commensurate authority to make decisions in carrying out the work. A personal assistant has no responsibility or authority except that derived from the person assisted. A person to whom work is properly delegated is responsible for its execution, and should have the necessary authority to make the decisions that are required in order to be effective. It is essential if people are to be motivated and developed that they know as precisely as possible what they are supposed to do, what responsibilities they carry and the limits of their authority, which should match those responsibilities. It is as unfair and unwise to employ a personal assistant and treat him as a manager without authority as it is to employ a manager and treat him as a personal assistant. The key words are 'wise delegation', and it demands the selection of personnel of the right calibre. It is, of course, implicit that the person delegating the work remains accountable for it to the client through his superior and partners. Delegation does not transfer accountability.

The main questions that arise are:

1 When to delegate.
2 What to delegate (and what not to delegate).
3 To whom to delegate.
4 How to delegate.

Ideally delegation should be planned well before the stage is reached when one is over-burdened by work, particularly where new staff will need to be recruited. It is a disservice to the client to postpone the additional cost until overwork necessitates action. Typical symptoms to be watchful for are:

1 Preoccupation with an excessive proportion of routine work that could be done by less skilled or experienced

people. A good maxim to apply as an indicative test is 'I should only do that which only I can do'.

2 The occurrence of frequent 'emergencies' during which routine work is disrupted or deferred.

3 Excessive delay in implementing clients' instructions. A danger point has been passed when it is the client who is most frequently taking the initiative in reviewing progress by chasing the practitioner.

4 Lack of time for training and keeping up to date or for adequate holidays.

Deciding what to delegate is a matter of judgement within each profession to ensure competence in handling clients' lives or property. It will be partly dictated by the optional or necessary qualification of assistants and technicians, and it introduces the important aspects of control, supervision and training.

It is necessary to list all activities, ideally based on careful notes taken over a period, in order to isolate those that can be delegated and grouped together to make a rational and interesting job specification or departmental function. The resulting specification needs to be visualised as a set of activities as well as assignments to be completed. This leads to the subject of to whom work should be delegated, which in turn raises the question of whether the organisation should be built around the available people or the people should be selected to fit a predetermined structure. A choice must be made between the growth of departments assisting individual partners or the creation of specialised groups or departments, or the size at which the former should evolve into the latter.

In a small firm the qualities and skill of the available people must obviously be the starting point, notwithstanding that in larger units it is accepted that the people should be selected to suit a predetermined structure. As a firm grows, its structure will need to change from an informal basis to a more formal one in order to avoid becoming unwieldy and to facilitate control. This formality will also be necessary if a central head office is to supply specialist support services to branches.

Designing the organisation

The total volume of work must be separated into jobs, and then, as the volume increases, the jobs can be subdivided into positions which perform identical functions with, perhaps, slight variations dictated by the work coming in or the experience of the holder. Ideally jobs are designed such that each activity is performed better because of the knowledge gained or skill exercised in performing the other tasks. A danger lies in designing jobs that are either repetitive and monotonous, on the one hand, or too chaotic and diverse, on the other. The former can dehumanise and the latter can be difficult to control and measure. In certain systems of mass production the productivity of the group is extended far beyond that of any individual in it, but this system can produce jobs that provide no satisfaction and consequently create resentment. In the same way departments may be set up along purely functional lines which satisfy the demands of logic but fall short of providing the interest necessary for bright and enthusiastic people. Recent experiments have shown that small cooperative teams that are able to display their performance and emphasise the contribution and mutual interdependence of their members have increased job satisfaction, efficiency and output.

The activities that are grouped to form a department must have the following characteristics:

1 An adequate volume of business.
2 Importance to the firm sufficient for isolation in terms of profit.
3 Identity — either traditional or newly created.
4 Clarity of and correlation between activities.
5 Clear reporting lines.
6 Undivided loyalties within the department and unity of purpose with the firm as a whole.

Having divided the work, the following should be checked:

1 That the responsibility for each assignment and client is clear-cut so that any failure or negligence will be assignable without doubt.
2 That the work and goals of each department and person within it is accurately defined and can be measured, and

that overlapping, duplication or gaps do not occur.

3 That people are not placed in a position where they serve two masters, especially if conflict could divide loyalty.

4 That the vertical lines of responsibility are clear.

5 That there is no confusion between staff functions and line management responsibility or between the role of a personal assistant and that of a manager.

6 That the span of responsibility of each manager is reasonable.

7 That the levels of authority are not excessive, leading to remoteness of management and bureaucratic control.

Summary

Planning and organisation are necessary to transform a firm's goals into achievements. The work of planning must be approached with the right attitude and the planner carefully selected for qualities of objective and positive thinking. The planning process has many beneficial effects, including the testing of the goals, scrutiny of resources and clarification of the stepping stones or events that lie ahead. It also provides basic information necessary for the preparation of budgets and may expose the danger of unforeseen losses. The importance of the work justifies a formal or semi-formal approach and delegation of detail work to a person with adequate time for its execution. The planner must have sufficient experience and an overview of the whole practice, and the work should be programmed and impetus maintained by control from the top. The work must involve those who will be responsible for its execution and take into account changes that may result from new technology or equipment.

The way in which a business is organised has considerable influence on its character as well as its efficiency. The ability to specialise and to delegate are essential to handle modern technology and administration. The grouping of activities that form jobs and of jobs that form departments decides the work content and influences the satisfaction to be derived from it. The designer of the organisation has the opportunity to ensure that responsibility for each client or job is clearly assigned and that errors do not occur because of duplication or gaps which lead to vague accountability. The highly personal nature of some professional work may necessitate departure from some recognised tenets, but this does not invalidate their usefulness as guidelines. The process of delegation, which requires decisions as to what to delegate, to whom and when, simultaneously clarifies responsibility and provides the job holder with the chance to display his ability. In designing the organisation it is possible to avoid the errors of too great a span of responsibility or the remoteness of management associated with excessive levels of authority. For these reasons the work of planning and thought devoted to organisations are investments of time that can yield high dividends and distinguish the progressive from the static firm.

Checklist – Chapter 3

PLANNING AND ORGANISATION

1 Are the overall objectives of the firm stated with sufficient clarity to form the basis of detailed planning?
2 Are the objectives stated in terms of performance and profitability?
3 What is the attitude of the partners and of management to planning?
4 If the planning function is absent, are the reasons given sound?
5 Are the plans expressed in such a way that subsequent performance can be measured against the goals?
6 Has past performance been analysed in sufficient detail for trends to be established?
7 Can the firm's goals be expressed as a series of realistic 'stepping stones' towards their attainment?
8 Does the firm's performance indicate a lack of planning, i.e. does it habitually suffer disruption through emergencies, work overload or rushed assignments?
9 Does the momentum in planning work come from the top?
10 Is the responsibility for planning clearly assigned?
11 Is adequate time allocated for planning work or does it habitually take second place to operational demands?
12 Is each operational department involved in the work?
13 Is the work of planning supported by adequate administrative resources?

14 To what extent should the planning work involve marketing activity?

15 To what extent will the firm's future strength depend on future activities, i.e. research and development, and are those responsible adequately included?

16 Is the person responsible for planning suitably forward-looking, open-minded and ambitious?

17 Does the firm monitor external influences that may affect its plans in sufficient detail to react positively to changes during the execution of the plan?

18 Are plans supported by budgets?

19 Are plans expressed in terms of future staff requirements?

20 Are plans critically examined by a person with sufficient experience who has not been involved in their creation?

21 To what extent may the firm's external advisers strengthen the planning process?

22 Does the plan include the future structure of the firm? How does the proposed organisation compare with other firms who have successfully achieved similar goals?

23 Is there any danger that the firm may be approaching future problems with solutions evolved to deal with past situations?

24 Does the plan properly recognise changes that will be caused by predictable advances in technology, law or procedure?

25 To what extent does the plan rely on re-training potentially obsolescent staff, and is the cost and realism of the process fully recognised?

26 If the firm is moving towards a more formal organisation, will any action be necessary to preserve the goodwill of existing clients?

27 Is work efficiently and effectively delegated?

28 Do any key personnel require training to improve delegation?

29 Has the total volume of work been analysed and grouped into sensibly related jobs and departments?

30 Will the planned organisation provide jobs of interest and could changes in organisation enrich work?

31 Can the performance of every department or function be measured?

32 Does the proposed organisation place any person in a position where his loyalties could be divided or his role obscured by conflict?

33 Is responsibility for each client clear-cut and are clients' affairs given the correct priority?

34 Is there any risk of confusion between staff and line functions?

35 Will any partners or managers be overtaxed by excessive spans of responsibility or workload?

36 Is there any danger that partners may become remote from the lower levels within the firm?

37 Is the planned organisation devised to give unity of purpose throughout the firm or is there any danger of fragmentation of interests?

'With what measure you mete it shall be measured to you.'

St Mark (4.24)

CHAPTER 4

Control and review

No one would think of building a machine without controls to start and stop it, to regulate its speed or direction and to make it perform according to the operator's wishes. A car with badly worn steering or a loose accelerator is a nightmare to drive. A business without adequate controls is an equally frightening thing to run. With things mechanical controls can be designed well in advance and high standards of precision achieved. When one comes to deal with human beings collaborating within the structure of an organisation, matters are not quite so straightforward, and this is the category into which most professional firms fall.

In industry one often finds control systems that are formalised and deal with all the aspects of importance to the company. A production control department may regulate output to ensure that delivery dates are met; a cost accounting department may monitor costs, and a quality control section may check quality. Such formalised systems, while providing consistent standards and speed, are often in conflict, and the manager will frequently be preoccupied with the reconciliation of quality, quantity and cost. This may even become the manager's prime function, and it emphasises the importance of the manager as a controller.

Control of the activities of a professional team is invariably a much more personal affair, often taking place during the actual execution of the work and perhaps largely a matter of professional judgement in each case. The extent to which controls can be automatic or formalised or must be personal is determined more by the nature of the activity than by choice. From this the following general conclusions may be drawn:

1 Every business must have controls if it is to be *in* control. They are important management tools.
2 They will vary according to the activity and must therefore be designed to suit each case.
3 Some will be devised for the management of the business as a business, and others will be primarily aimed to control assignments, that is for the protection or benefit of the client's interests or safety.
4 Controls frequently focus attention on conflicting demands and require judgement in those settling the final compromise.

The purpose of controls is to ensure that events take place in conformity with the adopted plan *or* standards of practice and with the general policy and procedure laid down. The word 'policy' refers to the written and unwritten rules to be followed in attaining objectives, and 'procedure' means the instructions given to people as to how and when to execute their work or how to handle contingencies that can be foreseen.

In determining their overall objectives, the partners must take a number of external influences into account, for example, the economy and technical progress. These are matters which are outside and beyond their control, but which influence performance and therefore come within the embrace of the subject. This paradox is clarified when one remembers that the word 'controls' is not the plural of the word 'control'. As Drucker points out*: 'The synonyms for controls are measurement and information. The synonym for control is

*Peter F. Drucker, *Management – Tasks, Responsibilities, Practices,* p 494, Heinemann.

direction.' Thus the former deals with past and current events and the latter with the future. Controls are concerned with the detection and measurement of significant external and internal events and trends and the latter with response and adjustment.

Designing controls

The design and operation of controls and the act of controlling a business are costs and the aim must be economy of means. In observing the external factors, some will be measurable and available in the form of published and reliable statistics, and the problem will be to select those that give significant information about the firm's environment. Prices too, as will be seen in the chapter on marketing, reveal a great deal about supply and demand, and the cost and availability of the resources of the supplier and consumer. However, there will be some trends, upon which management should form an opinion, that cannot be quantified, for example, shifts in public opinion, matters of fashion and political influences.

The measurement of internal events is temptingly simple and can too easily lead to misplaced emphasis on gathering rather than interpreting and using information. There are no hard and fast rules, and what is significant in one firm may have no meaning to another. Therefore each business must design controls and a control system appropriate to its activities and the speed with which it can go awry if it gets out of control. The following general guidelines are useful:

1 Controls should highlight results and focus attention on performance. For this reason gross fees and profits earned by the whole, by each department or from each service or client are commonly measured at monthly, quarterly and annual intervals, and their trends are essential information. The proportion of clients who could return and do not, the numbers that enlarge their brief after initial acquaintance — these are measures of achievement in building relationships with clients.

Costs of the firm as a whole and of each department or assignment are in themselves only numbers unless, by comparison; they indicate a rate of change or, expressed as a ratio, they are related to fees brought in. Stock figures are equally dreary expressed in isolation and do not assist control unless they are expressed in terms of performance or potential performance. Therefore the process of designing controls starts with the question 'What information can most economically and clearly inform us of our performance?' Measurement of the insignificant is a waste of money.

2 Measurement should only be to an accuracy that is necessary to grasp the desired meaning. Excessive analysis or accuracy blurs meaning and reduces impact. The designer must consider the method of quantifying statements that will give them clarity and impact.

3 Controls must produce information at a frequency and speed that permits adjustment in time. Companies in financial difficulties frequently discover the fact *too late* to remedy the situation. Some controls need to prompt action within minutes; for others weeks or even months may be adequate. The week, month, quarter and year, while convenient, should not be picked without thought. It may be more important to ensure that equal time periods are used for accurate comparison.

4 The designer should remember that controls influence the way people think, talk, act and react. Because they measure performance, they touch upon people's sensitivity and self-interest. It is quite common to encounter characters of crafty disposition who will act *against* the interests of the company in order to benefit themselves or their departments by the manipulation of controls, for example, by engaging in unnecessary expenditure to use up a budget. Thus there are occasions when performance and operational efficiency must be measured in preference to events.

5 A business is constantly changing either by design or response to a change in the character of work undertaken. Controls become obsolete unless they are regularly reviewed. Obsolete controls waste money and irritate the intelligent.

6 Controls should be appropriate to the level concerned and the controller. The amount of detail necessary at one level of supervision may be excessive at a higher level. Reported information should be limited to that which is really necessary for the controller's performance. This implies that partners should not be bogged down by detailed work that they should delegate.

Most activities require control and they include:

1 The work of design, engineering, production, adaptation and repair.
2 The provision of services and advice.
3 Buying, selling and exchange in trading or brokerage.
4 The use of fixed capital.
5 The use of working capital, e.g. cash creditors and debtors.
6 Manpower — cost, recruitment and manning levels.
7 Security and maintenance.
8 Marketing programmes and sales efforts.

But controls in themselves are useless unless they trigger an appropriate response in time for manoeuvre. This requires an organisation and control system that channels information to the right people at the right time; the recipients must also have the requisite authority to act without delay. This in turn reinforces the need for clarity in planning and organisation.

Effective control also demands discipline, for unless remedial instructions are acted upon, their effect is lost. Lax discipline saps control and may expose the firm to commercial dangers or the staff to safety hazards. Weak discipline undermining control has been identified as a contributory cause in many accidents, including those in such professional places as research laboratories.

Reference has already been made to the need for economy on the grounds of cost and the 'background noise' generated by control systems. This has brought about the most useful technique of control by exception. In this approach management concerns itself not with *what* is happening but with *variations* from plan. The degree of tolerable variance is predetermined in the planning stage, and action is only promoted when that tolerance is exceeded. Thus a clerical comparison is made between the plan and the reality without the use of management time, which only becomes involved when necessary or upon certain contingencies arising. This system can only function well if planning is realistic and controls are effective; false alarms will dull reactions.

While control is derived from planning, it is also an important source of feedback to the plan. The processes of planning, execution, coordination and control are, to an extent, cyclical. Departures from the plan may be remedied by corrective action, but they may equally expose a weakness or impossibility in the plan itself. In this case swift modification of the plan will be necessary in order that *all* the effects of the change may be understood. The repercussions of an error in the plan may extend far beyond the horizons of the person solving the immediate difficulty. Budgets may need alteration, contractual rights might need to be invoked, additional capital may be needed. Unless the departure is fed back *into the beginning of the process*, serious errors may be made by others unaware of the change. This is an inherent danger when a department 'covers up' a variance or distorts reports for purely sectional interests.

In critical areas, multiple controls may be necessary to reduce the risk of error to an absolute minimum. Controls themselves are not exempt from error, and duplicating or cross-checking controls may be necessary to secure peace of mind and safety. It is interesting to note that the process of natural selection has resulted in duplication of eyes, ears and hands, all essential controls with which to maintain body control and to survive.

The processes of measurement, evaluation, comparison with the plan, remedial action and follow-up all depend on communications (which form the subject of Chapter 7). Control cannot be maintained unless the communications system is sound and designed to accommodate the control system. They cannot be devised in isolation.

Situations arise where additional or special controls may be desirable. These include:

1 Projects of an unusually large size or unfamiliar nature for the firm.
2 Periods after the opening of new departments or branches

when control needs to be tighter and a sound statistical base is needed for future planning.

3 The early stages following mergers or takeovers when the process of adjustment is at work.
4 Periods of rapid expansion or those following relocation.
5 Times of financial stress or consolidation.
6 Times when new management or managers are establishing themselves and confidence in performance has not yet been attained.
7 Periods following the introduction of new technology, e.g. a computer, when the learning process needs more attention than usual and plans are being tested and feedback is essential.

These special short-term controls can be relaxed and diluted to form the routine system when the period of tension is over.

Some common errors in control

One risk that attends any change in the frequency, form or content of reports is the loss of comparability with past information. This in turn makes trends more difficult to study. For this reason changes in accounting methods, for example, the valuation of stock or work-in-progress, usually cause auditors or financial observers to look at the figures with great care and may hinder subsequent management.

Apart from internal management, a business can get out of control because it enters an 'open-ended' commitment. This is a danger of which every manager and executive should beware, particularly during times of inflation when a firm may be bound by contract to fulfill an obligation, while costs are rising through influences beyond its control.

Loss of control can also occur when the organisation imposes an excessive span of responsibility upon those in key places. Excessive work load inevitably leads to a situation where those demands which exert the most pressure are dealt with at the expense of those that demand the least. Should the neglected work take the form of a secondary management function such as coordination or supervision, then the firm enters an area of risk. It is worth remembering that excessive spans of responsibility are not always imposed by a bad organisation structure; they can be self-inflicted by a failure to delegate.

One final point on the subject of control is to recall the common error of doing too little too late. Underestimating the gravity or speed of events or overestimating the efficiency of remedial action, while often arising from excessive optimism, can signal sloppy controls, dull communications, or lack of will in those that manage.

Review

In the hurly burly of professional life it is natural that the incoming assignments quickly eclipse completed work. Indeed in considering management as a subject, great emphasis is laid on the future, and a good proportion of time is devoted to planning and conjecture. Nevertheless experience is of great value, and the review of achievement and error is essential to the advance of standards and the training of the younger members of a team. Business performance tends to crystalise into the figures on the balance sheet, and where lessons learnt are not recognised, they are a loss.

Meetings at all levels, specifically to review progress and exchange views, help to diminish the isolation of departments and provide an opportunity to discuss the intangible aspects of performance and client relations. In addition they help to avoid slavery to precedent, which is by no means unknown in some professional and business circles. Indeed such slavery can extend into all spheres, not least those of the forces too. 'The fascinating thing about life in military aviation is that there is always something new to be learnt. There are two basic and apparently paradoxical principles to be applied. Never forget the lessons of the past. Never re-apply them too rigidly to new circumstances. Either way disaster lies.'*

**A Lighter Shade of Blue*, Memoirs of Air Chief Marshal Sir Christopher Foxley-Norris, p 87, Ian Allen.

Summary

It has been said, though more often of large organisations than of small, that the business cycle consists of the following phases:

1 Enthusiasm for the next project.
2 Disillusionment when things turn sour.
3 Panic.
4 Search for the guilty.
5 Punishment of the innocent.
6 Praise and promotion for those not involved.

Now while this may be a cynical overstatement, it does illustrate the pattern of events where controls are inadequate, control is weak and where there is no procedure for review. Whether it is because management has failed to recognise that in human affairs things that can go wrong often do, or because they erroneously feel that controls are intrusive, matters little. The fact remains that controls, particularly when impersonal, reduce stress, increase objectivity, and focus attention on those activities that really matter for the health of thc whole firm. In the final analysis a manager who has failed to devise adequate controls is at best not in control and at worst out of control, at which level management becomes a spectator sport.

Checklist - Chapter 4

CONTROL AND REVIEW

1 Is the firm aware of the importance of control?
2 Is the difference between 'controls' and 'control' understood?
3 Does the nature of the work demand control as each assignment proceeds, and to what extent can impersonal controls be devised?
4 Apart from controls necessary for the business of the practice, what controls are desirable to ensure protection of the client's interests?
5 To what extent can the design of the control system be used to focus attention on the important areas of performance within the firm?
6 Are the business plans and organisations sufficiently clear for the design of a sound system of controls?
7 What controls are appropriate for sensing or measuring changes in the firm's environment which signal that a response is necessary?
8 Is the cost of controls recognised and is any money wasted in the collection of unnecessary or out of date information?
9 Is the balance between external and internal controls sensible?
10 Is the firm aware of all the available published statistics that may be useful in measuring performance?
11 What is the minimum information necessary to control the firm?
12 Is excessive mathematical accuracy or analysis wasting money or blurring reports?
13 Do reports provide an accurate and vivid picture of progress?

14 Is the frequency of reports appropriate to their purpose, and are they prepared in time for remedial action?
15 Are controls reviewed at regular intervals?
16 Is excessive detail rising too high in the organisation?
17 Have people receiving reports sufficient authority to act in the appropriate time scale?
18 Are there any opportunities for reducing cost and labour by introducing management by exception techniques?
19 Do controls feed back appropriate information for the amendment of plans?
20 Does the firm engage in any activities that merit special short-term controls to reduce risks?
21 Have any changes caused a loss of comparability between past and present performance?
22 Is there any risk of loss of control occurring through excessive spans of responsibility in key places?
23 Is there a formal review process and does it form a part of training?

'The first impression that one gets of a ruler and his brains is from seeing the men that he has about him.'

Machiavelli

CHAPTER 5

Personnel recruitment and selection

It is in personnel selection that a firm can get its largest advantage and through enlightened personnel administration that it can retain that advantage. The financial success of a firm is to a large extent determined by the success with which its management can match the skills of its human resources to the demands of the work brought in. Yet few firms allocate sufficient priority, time or funds to the recruitment, selection and administration of personnel.

In many cases the search for staff is only triggered by a resignation; selection is largely a matter of instinct, and administration is confined to salary negotiation, too often initiated by the employee. Whereas the larger company in commerce or industry can justify the cost of a formalised personnel management function, most smaller businesses regard it as an occasional task falling to one of the partners. The difficulty that arises is that neither capability in a professional subject nor the legal control of a business necessarily endows a person with skill in selecting and caring for people.

Whereas the industrialist may gain a long-term advantage from the development of a patentable or exclusive product or from the investment of capital in profitable plant or resources, the professional lives largely by his immediate reputation and prospers according to his personal skill and efficiency.

In some occupations a reputation may be based almost entirely on the success of the last assignment. Thus the effect of errors in selection or reduced vitality in a firm may quickly be felt.

The challenge that has to be faced by the founder of every business which hopes to grow in size is to get over the hurdle that separates the sole practitioner from the larger, more formalised organisations in which effective delegation is routine and efficient communications are established. Such organisations rely heavily on the selection of the right people because organisation, no matter how good, cannot compensate for lack of staff calibre. In business generally there is a tendency to concentrate too much on organisation and assets and not enough on the human resources employed.

Thus the professional, when acting as a manager, must achieve a high standard by recognising the importance of the process, planning the activity well and cultivating his understanding of people. Furthermore it must become an *integral* part of the management function and the thinking of all who manage.

The policy adopted by a firm for personnel matters should be the subject of regular review by the partners in the form of a written statement. The principals or managers responsible for its administration should undergo training, and the whole activity should be regulated so as to avoid inconsistencies in application. Policies should be devised to cover:

1 Organisation and general staffing levels.
2 Recruitment methods and selection procedures.
3 Terms of employment and salary scales.
4 Staff training and development.
5 Arrangements for retirement, pensions and redundancy.
6 Welfare arrangements in the case of prolonged sickness, bereavement or family difficulty.
7 The handling of grievances, disciplinary matters and severance.

The influence of a changing society

The changes that have taken place in society over the last

century are as influential as those in technology. The relationship between employer and employee is no exception. It is easy to forget how far it has evolved from the warehouse of Murdstone and Grimsby that so numbed young David Copperfield, as each step in the advance is so quickly taken for granted. The process has not yet been completed; it is spurred on by the desire of the individual for material progress, the restricted supply of and growing demand for skilled people, the rising level of general education and the perpetual stimulation of the media. However, despite these advances it remains an area in which there is a need for further development and an improved initiative by management. The professions have generally held themselves aloof from the unhappy labour relations in industry, and rightly so, but they are no less involved. The fragmented nature of much professional employment and the personal relationships existing between most partners and their staff have not been conducive to the organisation of labour. Times may change.

However, where large employers exist and labour can be organised, the pattern of industry has been followed, sometimes with damaging results. The professions as a whole, the bodies that govern them and the individual employers should take great pains to develop standards that represent a true advance on those that have brought so much loss to industry. In some professions the signs indicate that standards are no better than in industry and that where labour can be organised, the too familiar story is repeated. Additionally the professions often find that they are in competition with industry and central and local government for staff. Consequently the terms that they must offer are dictated by the opportunities for the skilled as a whole and not by the economies within the profession. This competition has become international and further enhanced by tax advantages of overseas employment. The private practitioner may find that he is competing with government and industry both at home and overseas, and this is a trend more likely to grow than to diminish.

Labour relations are the inescapable responsibility of management, and the cost of lost initiative or leadership far outweighs the price of its retention. The foundation of intelligent personnel management is a sensitivity to changes in society and the needs of people as employees. It is only upon such an understanding that the process can be successfully integrated into the daily routine of management.

Manpower planning

Because the process of recruitment and selection may span months, management must anticipate its needs by planning. In the larger firm, departments and branches will have previously agreed requirements for staff according to the income they are expected to generate and the type of work they hope to carry out. The 'establishment', as the agreed labour force is sometimes called, should define each job and the number of positions for each job.

If the establishment is not thought out and controlled, or is left to different departmental heads, the use of manpower will become uneven and may vary from the parsimonious to the extravagant. Labour is the greatest individual item of cost to a firm and must be kept in an acceptable ratio to the gross fees earned. Thus the completion of a budget necessitates manpower forecasting, as does the comparison of future profitability in different areas of activity.

In many firms there will be relatively few fluctuations in staffing needs, as the incoming volume of work may be comparatively stable, but this is by no means universal. For example, small firms associated with the building industry may be subject to considerable fluctuations, perhaps to the extent of creating special teams for specific projects. Seasonal changes may also occur, for example, in handling peak loads caused in accounting by the end of tax years or in medicine by winter ailments.

The cause of vacancies

The need for staff may arise for a number of reasons:

1 Retirement, illness or death.
2 Staff leaving voluntarily or beause of severance.

3 Promotion.
4 Job creation by:
   a expansion,
   b advancing technology, or
   c changing type of work undertaken, e.g. diversification.
5 Changes in organisation.

Whereas occasionally vacancies occur through wholly unexpected reasons, the majority of cases should be foreseen. The cost of an unfilled vacancy or change in staff may be high and arise through:

1 Loss of output and therefore income.
2 Loss of productivity by new people taking over existing cases.
3 Possible loss of clients and discontinuity in work undertaken.
4 Training and re-training costs.
5 Possible loss of other staff.

The period for which a vacancy remains effectively unfilled will vary but will comprise the time necessary to do the following:

a Draft and order advertising and contact other sources.
b Schedule and interview applicants.
c The time necessary for the selected person to disengage from his current employment and establish himself in the new position.

Senior staff may be bound under their existing contracts of employment to give lengthy notice, and where a new appointee is relocating his home further delays may occur. Where the employee is to go overseas delays could increase even more.

Preliminaries to recruitment

Before active recruiting can commence, it is important to prepare a definition of the vacancy to be filled and the qualifications and personal qualities of the ideal person to fill it. No matter how well the person responsible for recruitment may know the details, this is best done by the preparation of two written statements:

1 *The job description*, which defines the duties and responsibilities involved, i.e. a comedian to make people laugh, and
2 *The job specification*, which defines the qualities and skills necessary, i.e. self-confidence and a sense of humour and an ability to make people laugh.

It is termed an occupation, i.e. bank clerk or solicitor's managing clerk, where the type of work is well known and the job differs mainly in location, specialisation or terms of employment. However, there are other jobs or special tasks where the work cannot be defined by reference to an occupation because it has been evolved or has not yet become a standard or widespread activity.

In defining each job the following points should be borne in mind:

1 The organisation of a person's work has considerable influence over the satisfaction to be derived from its execution. The person to whom he is accountable and the activities for which he is responsible must be clear if stress or conflict is to be avoided. Each job must carry with it sufficient authority for the work to be executed properly.

2 Each job confers a degree of status both within the business and socially, and it has an appropriate array of status symbols. These include:

a The job title, authority.
b The office, space or accommodation and its exclusivity.
c Car size and type.
d Security.
e Length of holiday.
f Potential for advancement.

People are generally sensitive to their terms of employment and well aware of these symbols whether admitted or not. They are quick to resent what they believe to be inconsistent or unfair distribution of benefits or rank. Pecking order is a reality that it is unwise to forget.

Job descriptions

A job may be simplified in order to attract people who are available and to derive benefits analogous to mass production or reduce the amount of training needed. However, excessive simplification of duties can dehumanise a job and lead to resentment. Job enrichment, by the addition of duties not previously part of the job, can boost morale, increase efficiency and sometimes lead to a reduction in staffing levels. Most organisations are designed to maximise output. However, there is traditionally far too little attention to the satisfaction to be derived from a job and the challenge and variety of activity that it affords. Employees should both understand and feel their involvement in the firm and within their team.

Duties that have to be undertaken are aggregated to make a 'job'. Where the volume of work to be done exceeds the capacity of one person, then several 'positions' are created, each handling identical duties. Relatively small variations in the duties can produce change and avoid drudgery, always provided they are not distributed at random, which can be unsettling.

Unless the duties comprised in a job are clear, it is hard to devise controls that will measure or check performance. Similarly good performance cannot be demonstrated and recognised, which is important for the individual, especially in the professions. For these reasons it is desirable to review job descriptions at regular intervals. The act of preparing written descriptions helps to avoid the perpetuation of jobs which are obscure or ambiguous and helpful in recruiting, because it is the basic document from which advertising may be prepared, interviewing conducted and salaries assessed. It should describe:

1 The job title, grade, statutory or desirable qualifications, experience and location.
2 The person to whom and the persons for whom the job holder is responsible.
3 The purpose of the job and work comprised in it, including the degree of supervision and initiative necessary.

4 The responsibilities of the job and such features as client contact.
5 Details of any specialised apparatus, equipment or procedures with which the job holder must be familiar.
6 Any particular features such as the need to work unusual hours or to travel at short notice that may eliminate certain candidates.

Job specifications

This sets out the necessary skills and personal qualities, such as the following:
1 Training and qualifications.
2 Experience and postgraduate achievement.
3 Character and such personal qualities as:
  a Leadership.
  b Manner and ability to handle people.
  c Power of expression and communication.
  d Appearance.
  e Stability, motivation and drive.
  f Ability to accept responsibility and to delegate.

In undertaking this work it is necessary to visualise the candidate through the eyes not only of the employer but of his subordinates, colleagues and clients.

The examining bodies make a vital contribution in ensuring a predetermined and consistent standard of technical knowledge. The respect of the public is largely retained by this examination. However, qualification neither ensures a person's suitability for a particular job nor casts much light upon his character or industry in his mature years.

As technology advances a person may quickly lose touch with the latest developments if he does not continue with postgraduate training, and the assumption of administrative duties may further reduce contact with his original discipline. A job specification should state the importance of a person's current knowledge as well as his examination successes. Having completed these studies, the employer should be in a position where he thoroughly understands the current work to be done and the skills necessary to achieve his standards. He will also have reviewed the relevance of the position within the organisation and the financial effects of the job in the terms of the profit and loss account. Only when this is done should he proceed to the next step, that of recruitment.

Recruitment

The larger the number of applicants considered for a position the greater are the opportunities for success in selection. A common error in recruiting is inadequate expenditure of time and effort. A disappointing result is all too frequently attributed to a general shortage of staff, when in reality the budget has been quite out of proportion to the importance of the matter and the true cost of an error. Inadequate scale of expenditure or effort must not only diminish the chances of getting the best person in each case but also, by cumulative effect, reduce the quality of the firm as a whole. In other cases the expenditure is adequate but unwisely spent.

Sources of staff

The sources of new staff are:

1 Internal, by transfer or promotion.
2 Advertising.
3 Agencies and bureaux and professional bodies.
4 Referrals and casual applications.
5 Competitors.
6 Schools and colleges, government bureaux and training centres.

1 Internal There will be occasions where there are no suitable internal candidates for a vacant position. However, unless opportunities exist for promotion, or the development of a person's ability by changes in his work, the group must not only face the prospect of always seeking staff externally, but also of its staff leaving in search of advancement or wider experience. It is equally true that the movement of staff among firms may be beneficial. The smaller firm may acquire specialists without the cost of training by offering a more informal atmosphere to people working in large and more impersonal units. At the same time, the individual may enjoy a greater variety of work in the family practice than he would in the large city firm. These might be quite proper stages in career development. The large firm is not necessarily the loser by the occasional injection of staff from the smaller unit. The error occurs when outside staff are taken on primarily to avoid embarrassment caused by internal promotion, thus unsettling all the existing staff who may have been working for advancement. Real or imagined disloyalty by the employer to his staff can be demoralising and increase staff turnover. Ideally staff should be selected and trained for internal promotion or reassignment to the mutual benefit of both employer and employee, and frankness will be necessary to avoid resentment where internal candidates are passed over. The first place to look for staff is therefore within the firm itself.

2 Advertising Advertising is the most costly but, at the same time, the most valuable method of attracting staff where it is judged that the widest number of prospects should be canvassed.

Different professions tend to use different types of newspapers or journals:

a National daily and Sunday newspapers.
b Regional evening papers.
c Local weekly newspapers.
d Generally circulated professional and technical magazines.
e The privately circulated magazine of professional bodies.

It is easy to waste money advertising in the wrong place or by inserting inadequate material that lacks in appeal. A study should be made of all likely newspapers and journals, the types of vacancies they announce and the rates that they charge. If the advertiser is inexperienced, it is worthwhile talking to similar firms or organisations to sound out their knowledge.

3 Agencies and bureaux The extent to which specialist employment agencies have developed varies a lot from profession to profession. The satisfaction expressed with the services they provide also varies greatly. As with most professions much will depend on the clarity of understanding achieved with the client. Generally the employment bureau enjoys the following advantages over the individual employer:

a A wider view and knowledge of the supply and demand for labour that comes with daily involvement in recruitment and selection.

b As ability to compare terms and conditions offered by different clients.

c Greater skills developed by regular involvement.

d The maintenance of registers of known vacancies and candidates, enabling them to achieve introductions without specific advertising.

e A greater opportunity to compare the effectiveness of different types of advertising and the quality of candidates coming from different sources.

These are substantial advantages and more than justify the fees charged, providing the services are used intelligently and the bureau can also contribute advice in the development of general personnel policies, particularly in setting appropriate salary levels and general terms of employment. Most professional bodies maintain employment registers that should not be forgotten.

4 Referrals Unsolicited applications usually result from an unknown third party, recommendation or the reputation of the firm. They have the possible advantage of demonstrating the applicant's keenness and the suitability of the location of the employer, but unless the firm is large, the chances of matching a vacant job description at a particular moment must be remote. Where a candidate of desirable quality applies and there is no matching vacancy there will be a strong temptation to distort the organisation by the creation of an unplanned position or, worse, an unnecessary job. Nevertheless referrals are an excellent source, especially where they come from a reliable intermediary, and they can be stimulated in those cases where there is a well-developed 'grapevine' for unofficial communication among firms in the same profession. Participation by principles and staff in the local affairs of their institute or association also tends to increase their knowledge of suitable local talent and to attract it where their organisation is of good local standing.

5 Competitors The deliberate solicitation of staff of a competing firm, popularly known as 'headhunting', may be an attractive way of securing people of known calibre with an added bonus that it simultaneously weakens the competitor, but it is considered by many to be a malpractice. However, it is a matter of degree and influenced by the directness or remoteness of the competition and the size of the community, both social and professional, involved. One must also consider the possibility of obtaining confidential information or access to clients in such a way as to constitute an unfair advantage over a fellow practitioner. Borderline cases inevitably arise and it is a matter of judgement in each case, perhaps best guided by the general principle of doing unto others as you would have them do unto you.

6 Schools and colleges The relationship between schools and colleges and the local professional practices is all too frequently ignored by the parties concerned. Every opportunity should be taken by professional people to meet the young and explain their work to them, and equally schools should be aware of the local professional community and the career prospects that it provides. It is easy for the teaching and professional world to view each other from their respective ivory towers. A review of the calendar of functions of most leading professional bodies will quickly reveal the scant attention paid to the development of young people. For the recruitment of junior entrants there is no better source than referrals from teachers of tried ability in assessing their pupils. It is equally pleasing to find firms where some juniors come from the same school and thereby enjoy a continuation of the association that they developed during their education.

At the more advanced levels any senior staff who lecture on a part-time basis should be encouraged to work in close liaison with those responsible for recruitment, for they too will be far better able to spot talent than the interviewer dealing with unknown applicants responding to newspaper advertisements.

The selection of personnel

The selection of staff is one of the most fundamental activities undertaken by management. The capability, character and internal harmony of a firm is largely influenced by the selection of its people. It is a difficult process for it involves the judgement by one human being, hindered by his own prejudices and inhibitions, of another, who is probably attempting to conceal his.

Selecting the most suitable candidate to fill a vacancy involves matching the required and available ability, aptitude and character. Some compromise is inevitable in the final decision. People differ and the assessment is a matter of judgement, unaided by any precise measurement. It is inevitably a procedure in which standards vary from 'hunch' and guesswork to sophisticated techniques that would baffle a psychiatrist. It is sadly a procedure which frequently falls short of desirable standards and leads at best to dull performance and at worst to disillusionment — faults occasionally compounded by nepotism.

The benefits that follow from successful selection justify emphasis; they include:

1 Improved value of service to the clients or patients of the firm, leading to improved reputation of the practice.
2 Higher staff morale leading to reduced labour turnover, lower induction and training costs and more soundly based loyalties of the firm to its staff and the staff to the firm.
3 Improved internal efficiency and communication by the avoidance of weak links and discordant members of the team, leading to enhanced job satisfaction and internal harmony.
4 Improved employer-employee relationships, all of which in turn lead to:
5 Improved profitability and greater satisfaction to the proprietors in the running of their business.

In a process that offers such rewards, every effort to eliminate or reduce the risk of error is justified. This is best achieved by working carefully in accordance with a predetermined system. The stages are:

a Preparing for the selection process.
b Analysis of the applications and the shortlisting of candidates for the preliminary interview.
c The preliminary interview and shortlisting for the second interview.
d The final selection or main interview.
e Selection and negotiation of terms.

For the purpose of this discussion it is assumed that the appointment is of sufficient importance to merit two interviews.

(a) *Preparing for the selection process*

1 Choosing the interviewer In many commercial organisations the first screening of applicants, both internal and external, is carried out by a specialist personnel department. Those that are 'shortlisted' are then interviewed by the manager or person to whom they will be answerable. Where employees number hundreds, such a department is essential. In the smaller professional firm such sophistication is impractical. Nevertheless the process remains the same, though preliminary and final interviewing may be carried out by the same person. What is important is that the person interviewing should have studied the techniques, prepared for the meeting thoroughly and have demonstrated an ability in assessing people. It is both undesirable and dangerous to select staff and then, as it were, to 'issue' them to people who may then find them unsatisfactory or incompatible.

A variety of solutions may be satisfactory. In the small firm the preliminary screening and administration may be done by one partner and the selection by two. Clerical staff may be dealt with by a senior secretary subject to a final selection by a partner. In the larger concern the partnership secretary may undertake the preliminary work. In other cases the administration of the process may be carried out by a senior partner's secretary, the first shortlisting by the manager or technician involved and the final selection by the manager and partners concerned. In so personal a unit as a professional firm, where the principals are accountable and legally liable to their clients, it is essential that appointments should be the concern of the partners.

2 *Interpretation of the job description and job specification, and preparation for the interview* The first task of the interviewer is to interpret the job description and job specification. If he is not personally acquainted with the duties of the job, he should discuss it with the present holder of a similar position or the immediate supervisor. The interviewer will need to formulate key questions, the replies to which will reveal the suitability of the candidate. It is unlikely that such questions can be thought of on the spur of the moment, and in any case it is better for the interviewer to leave his mind free to listen, to observe the applicant and to make notes on the answers for later consideration.

The interview is concerned with three aspects:

(i) The candidate's technical knowledge.
(ii) The person's motivation and relationship with his work.
(iii) The candidate's intelligence, personality and his likely relationship with the existing staff.

Technical knowledge In the majority of professions, technical knowledge and, it is usually assumed, competence, are demonstrated by qualification. The general public and practitioners alike rely on the examining authority. It should be a relatively easy matter to decide upon the appropriate qualifications. However, essential though qualifications may be, they by no means reveal enough upon which to base a selection. A person's experience, what he has gained from that experience and his ability to apply that knowledge are all different questions that confront the interviewer. He should search his mind for past errors of his own, or of staff in the same job, from which he can frame questions that will reveal the candidate's learning level from experience. Some people may gain ten years' knowledge from ten years' work, unhappily others may only gain one year's experience ten times over.

For those who are in rapidly advancing technologies or engaged with such subjects as taxation or changing areas of the law, it may almost be a full-time job to keep their knowledge up-to-date. Questions may be necessary to probe the candidate's postgraduate studies, both formal and private, to confirm that his current knowledge is adequate. It can occur that the person responsible for interviewing is not personally able to assess the technical competence of the candidate, in which case assistance or external advice should certainly be taken. It is also from the desired level of experience that the interviewer will form an opinion on the preferred age group of the candidate.

The qualifications, experience and knowledge of a person are perhaps the easiest aspects to judge; it is when one comes to matters of character — that is, the person's stability, personality, motivation and temperament, in short, his will and ability to apply his knowledge and to get on well with clients and colleagues — that measurement and certainty of judgement become more difficult and subjective. In consequence this is the area where most of the mistakes are made which lead to disappointment by the employers in their chosen staff.

Motivation The quality of a person's work, the volume of his output, the contribution that he makes to the team and his relationship with his clients are largely coloured by his personal motivation. An employer may encourage staff by designing both an organisation and individual jobs that satisfy, and a reward system that stimulates, but the mainspring remains within individuals and varies in strength accordingly. The degree to which they initiate their own progress, the intensity of their personal drive, and the inbuilt needs for which they seek satisfaction all influence their work. As such they concern the employer. Those choosing staff should consider the level of motivation appropriate to the job. To recruit the ambitious to a routine work with little opportunity for real advancement is to err as badly as to appoint a person of academic skill and little ambition to a post requiring drive.

Desire alone does not decide a person's effectiveness. His self-confidence, degree of introversion or extroversion and no less his intelligence will also decide the final result. The questions asked should be designed to draw out information that will cast light on a person's basic motivation, his stability and his intelligence. Competition in the professional world is not usually as strong as it is in the spheres of commerce and industry. Consequently the competitive spirit is often underdeveloped or even totally lacking in or frowned upon by some professionals. The attitude that it is the game that matters and not who wins may not be in the best interests of the younger or expanding professional practice. Thus a person's competitive spirit and commercial awareness merit scrutiny. This is especially the case where the professional work involves him in acting for clients in contentious or litigious matters, for example, where success demands confidence, boldness or even audacity to back professional skill.

Intelligence and personality The speed with which a person can grasp a situation, often incompletely or ineptly explained, can be a talent of the greatest importance in the professional world. In many cases a client may consciously or subconsciously distort facts upon which judgement must be based. The need for such talents in a particular job must be matched by the intelligence of the job holder. Where it is not, then artful clients will quickly reduce the knowledgeable but perhaps naive professional to a miserable state of confusion.

Under this heading may conveniently be considered the need for the holder of a particular job to communicate well. How essential the ability is will vary, but it is likely to be of importance in most cases. The accuracy and speed with which opinions may be exchanged or further advice taken or clients advised may go to the root of an individual's efficiency. It may have a bearing on the speed with which he can secure a client's confidence. At times when a client or patient becomes confused or demoralised, concise expression of clear thinking can do much to restore order. Each interviewer must therefore decide the standard of communication that he is looking for in the candidate's ability to express himself, to listen and understand.

Another matter of importance in dealing with people's personal and sometimes embarrassing problems is the adviser's sympathy and empathy and, even greater, his ability to avoid the error of confusing the two. A varying affinity to different clients always exists, but work usually demands objectivity and the avoidance of personal identification with a client's problems. This by no means rules out the value of the ability to project one's personality into, and so to understand, a client's real needs, while relating them to one's discipline and not to emotions.

In some cases a complete match of all characteristics between the job and the candidate, which in itself would be quite remarkable, would lead to failure if the candidate lacked originality. If innovative flair is an important talent for the work, then the interviewer must bring to the meeting a clear idea of the way in which such talent may have been demonstrated. Every interviewer should study the contacts that the job holder will maintain and the type of personality necessary to handle them. Externally the most important will probably be the clients; internally the balance of a team may have to be considered, as well as the candidate's capacity for command or leadership. The integrity needed both to do justice to the work, the firm and the profession should not escape assessment. It may be indicated by voluntary work in professional organisations and the intensity of vocational feeling.

A job description and specification are guides to the interviewer but no more. His success will depend on the depth of his understanding. The interviewer must have a clear idea of the weight that he attaches to each characteristic if he is to avoid being deflected by a particular candidate's individual appeal or talents that may be distinguished but inappropriate.

(b) Analysis of the applications

The object at this stage is to select those applicants that seem suitable for interview. A poor result may necessitate further or altered advertising if the process is really to be one of selection.

Where the vacancy has been described well and perhaps amplified by a mention of the type of job and salary that a suitable person will at present be commanding, the number of inappropriate applications should be few. Nevertheless there is often an element which is doomed to fail at this early stage for a number of reasons, often one of the following:

1 Badly written letters.
2 Letters that display, even at this stage, an unacceptable,

off-hand or hostile attitude to employment.

3 The submission of details of experience that might be unsuitable or with firms from which it is undesirable to attract staff.

(c) The preliminary interview

It is assumed that the appointment is one of sufficient seniority to merit at least two interviews. Some people believe that a minimum of two interviews should precede any appointment, as people change from day to day to a considerable extent, both as interviewers and interviewees. First impressions are not always confirmed at subsequent meetings. The candidates also benefit from two interviews, for it gives them the opportunity to think about the job disclosed at the first meeting and perhaps to take the advice of friends; it also enables questions to be thought out and enhances the confidence with which they approach the main meeting.

The following administrative matters should be dealt with before the meetings take place:

1 The length of each interview. The interviewer's diary should be arranged to allow completely uninterrupted sessions. It is unlikely that there can be less than half an hour for each person.

2 The number of people to be interviewed consecutively. The most experienced people can become confused if they see too many people in quick succession. To interview more than four or five people in a morning will hardly allow enough time between seeing each person for making notes or for reflection on the answers to the questions.

3 Travel arrangements for the candidates. The distance each applicant has to travel will vary, and those with the shortest distance should be interviewed at the earlier times. A policy should be agreed for the payment of travel and out of pocket expenses if appropriate.

4 There are few more unsettling experiences than to arrive late for an interview. Each invitation should confirm when and where the interview is to be held and give directions on how to get there from a well-known land-

mark. The receptionist should be told the names of expected candidates, and suitable waiting facilities should be available. In short every candidate should be accorded the same courtesy as a new client.

The preliminary interview should be planned to elicit the information in a reasonably speedy and straightforward way. While many people dislike application forms, they are useful providing they are simple and confine themselves to important facts about education, career pattern and personal details.

Interviews usually fall into one of two types — those where the proceedings are tightly controlled, for example by adherence to a questionnaire, and those where the candidate is encouraged to range freely in his conversation. For the preliminary interview the controlled discussion will probably occupy most time, as the interviewer's first task is to get basic facts. Typically this information will be:

Personal details

Surname and christian or forenames and any former name.
Address and phone number.
Age and date of birth.
Marital status.

Education

Primary education.
Secondary education and examinations passed and failed.
Details of languages spoken and their fluency.
Universities or colleges with the dates of attendance and details of examinations passed and failed.
Professional training and the names of any previous employers providing practical experience during the training period.
Details of professional examination success and any other courses subsequently attended or private study.
Membership details of professional bodies.

Experience

The names of past employers and the duration of employment.

Details of job held, a general description of the type of experience gained and of achievements.
Information regarding job changes and promotion with each employer.
Reasons for leaving or for wishing to leave.
Position in the organisation, the person to whom they reported and the people reporting to them.
Current salary.

Social

Details of any principal outside activities or hobbies.

References

The names of three referees, provided that they will not be approached without the candidates' prior consent.

Driving licence

Details of driving licence if this is necessary for the performance of the work or consideration by the firm's insurers.

The interviewer should prepare suitable questions according to the vacancy. Finally he should round off the interview with a general description of the firm and the vacancy and an invitation to ask any questions. The resulting questions asked should be noted as they may reveal the uppermost thoughts in the candidate's mind.

At this stage, although conclusions may already be forming, the object is to decide whether or not to invite the applicant to a further interview, which will be in greater depth. If premature conclusions are drawn, they may bias the final assessment.

At the end of the meeting, and certainly before interviewing the next candidate and risking confusion, the interviewer should make notes on the following additional points:

1 The candidate's general bearing.
2 His level of self-confidence.
3 The suitability and style of his dress.
4 His apparent health.
5 The clarity and quality of the candidate's voice and ease of communication and comprehension.

6 Level of enthusiasm displayed.
7 The features of the job that interested the applicant.
8 The interviewer's impression on how the person would fit into the existing team.

Upon completion of this study candidates can be divided into three categories:

1 Unsuitable.
2 Marginal.
3 Suitable for the main interview.

Whether or not the marginal candidates go on to the main interview will largely depend on the number of candidates considered suitable.

(d) The main interview

The purpose of the main interview is to get to know the applicant in greater depth, or as much depth as possible within the limitations of a formal exchange. In many cases the interview will be conducted by two people, and a discussion should take place before the meeting to establish how the interviewers are to share the work.

Whereas the first meeting may have been tightly controlled, it is likely that more will be gained on the second occasion if the conversation is allowed to wander. It is therefore important that joint interviewers should establish a relaxed atmosphere and avoid anything approaching the nature of a cross-examination. If it is desirable to test the candidate's reaction to pressure, for example in assessing a salesman's resistance to an abrasive prospect, it is probably best left to the end of the interview. The candidate should be put at his ease, seated comfortably, and interruptions should be kept to a minimum.

Early background It is pleasant to start with the candidate's family background. The occupation of the parents and the careers followed by brothers, sisters and children illuminate the person's family influences. In understanding a person, knowledge of a 'broken home' or other early difficulty is helpful. An individual's progress in and attitude towards his basic education are also enlightening, including both examinations passed and the favoured and disliked subjects with his reasons for liking or disliking them. The clarity of his answers will reveal the degree of self-assessment with which he habitually thinks, though it is fair to remember that young people often respond to their teachers as much or even more than to the subject taught. Early hobbies, being freely chosen, may point to natural aptitudes, and achievement in individual or team sports are themes that merit discussion.

Further education and career selection The reasons for choosing a career are often, and surprisingly, something of a mystery. For some it is a matter of parental guidance; for others it may be the influence of fashion combined with a vague feeling of opportunism. At the other extreme there are those fortunate few whose imaginations are ignited by their first encounter with a particular subject, and where the zeal continues they usually achieve leadership or even eminence in their calling.

The compass of a person's study in relation to the set subjects for qualification and the range of postgraduate reading do much to indicate the extent to which qualification or success was seen as an objective. An unfortunate result of concentration on examination success is that for some it becomes an end in itself and not the means to an end. The personal effort displayed in achieving qualification may be significant. The mature candidate who passed exams by attendance at evening classes or by correspondence courses may value his progress more highly than a person who travelled by a more comfortable route.

Career development There is no finer evidence of a person's capability than the progress of his career. Actual accomplishments are the most eloquent references a person can bring to an interview and certainly the most reliable guide to his likely performance.

In the same way that a sound business will have a clear policy and plan for its future, so too should the individual in the matter of his career. This will be seen by the progressive nature of each change of job and the soundness of the reasoning behind a person's motives for change — this may all reveal anything from an opportunistic desire for advancement to a carefully worked strategy. This is not to decry enterprise; often the best opportunities come from the most unlikely quarters at unexpected moments, and good luck is as frequently the meeting of opportunity and preparedness as it is of chance.

However, changes of employment may also reveal a lack of central purpose, especially when justified by the unfortunate choice of a series of disappointing employers. Some people have an unhappy knack of choosing jobs which fail to live up to their expectations, and such patterns might mirror their own inadequacies. It is always interesting to learn what a person liked and disliked about a certain job, and it is useful for the interviewer to ask himself if the job he is offering will avoid these past difficulties. Inevitably mistakes are made by employers and employees. A series of brief and formal meetings cannot produce certainty, especially where both parties are in a negotiating stance. Past errors may be perfectly reasonable; it is a matter of degree and repetition and of listening thoughtfully to the answers.

It is in the realm of future career development that the meeting should become a dialogue rather than an interview. The prospective employer must obtain an idea of the candidate's ambitions and judge his ability to accommodate them. He must be candid and accurate in describing the work and the firm's policy for internal promotion and training. A person's career is a matter of very great importance, and success is not the filling of a vacancy but the formation of a mutually beneficial relationship. Such matters as a prospective employee's desire to gain wider experience, to specialise, to engage in research, to assume greater responsibility (or even less) should be discussed to a point of real understanding.

Character, personality and appearance While each member of a team must be agreeable to those people with whom he works, it must be remembered that those in contact with clients will condition the client's opinion of the firm as a whole. Social manner, social contacts and outside interests can be very important. The practice of meeting the wives or husbands (or friends) of candidates, sometimes viewed with horror as an intrusion into privacy, is sound. In many cases it should be regarded as essential. Many professional careers are almost impractical without the involvement and contribution of a person's partner in marriage. The final selection in such cases should not be made until a meeting, preferably informal, has given both parties a better chance to get to know each other.

(e) Selection

If the interviewers are fortunate the choice may be self-evident. On one occasion known to the writer a candidate with an unusual and ideal blend of experience, chosen unanimously by a panel, proved to be an alcoholic. It is more likely that different candidates will have varying appeal on different aspects. One may have an excellent personality and, perhaps, a patchy career; another may have demonstrated skill and an unfortunate manner. It is at this point that the preparation and thoroughness of the procedures bring their rewards, as the interviewers discuss the weight they attach to each facet of the job and the prospective job holder. The level of this debate will disclose the real skill of the proceedings and the objectivity of the final deductions. Having reduced the risk of error to a minimum, the final decision will be one of personal judgement, the quality of which management procedures are intended to cultivate rather than to replace.

Summary

The quality and success of a firm is to a large extent determined by the skill with which management selects its staff. Few firms are of a size that can afford a specialist personnel manager, and it is therefore important that the partner assuming this responsibility should give the work sufficient priority and time to ensure high standards. The damage that can occur when the employer loses the initiative in this vital area of management has been demonstrated by industry, and the professions must develop skills that will secure them against similar misfortunes and maintain a sound competitive base in an era of growing demand for skilled people.

Having started the process by recognising the importance of the subject and creating a sound policy that will avoid inconsistencies, the firm must formulate plans for meeting foreseen staff requirements that will allow adequate time for well organised recruitment and selection. This involves recognition of all the causes of vacancies so that they may be anticipated, and the examination of plans that may bring expansion or changes in the quality or skill of staff to undertake future work. The creation of job descriptions and specifications are essential prerequisites if the firm is to evolve as an organisation and avoid the possible error of expansion around individual talents. Study of every occupation within an organisation is also necessary to ensure that the work is varied, interesting and develops the job holder. Regular review is necessary in order to detect changes in the supply and demand for different specialists, as both flexibility and re-training in employment will become features of growing importance as progress in technology accelerates in future years. Both employers and employees, in fact all society, must recognise that a career in one unchanging occupation is a rapidly declining possibility.

The probability of success is largely determined by the number of applicants interviewed. Consequently the scale of recruitment effort, often inadequate, must be matched to the importance of the job *and* current market conditions, for the professions may be in competition with industry, commerce, government and employers overseas. The content of advertising can be more important than the size of the advertisement, and the use of bureaux, referalls, and good relations with educational establishments must all be explored.

The selection process requires both patience and skill, and careful inquiry combined with reflection are necessary to avoid the errors so common when people rely on instinct. The judgement of personal qualities is far harder than the assessment of technical ability which can usually, but not invariably, be deduced from the candidate's qualification and experience. Further, the personal qualities sought in the candidate must be thought out in creating the job specification.

The process of interview must be planned, and the interviewer must bring to the meeting a clear idea of the work to be done and the weight he attaches to the various activities and talents that he may encounter or uncover. The process is one that merits the maintenance of good records, and there are few appointments that do not justify assessment of the candidate by at least two people working to a well thought out plan.

The exploration of a person's career development, aptitudes, strengths, weaknesses and character require tact and a relaxed atmosphere. If they should be revealed later either as a pleasant surprise or a disappointment, then management has probably fallen short in one of its most important and fundamental skills, that of matching people to the challenge it creates for them.

Checklist — Chapter 5

PERSONNEL RECRUITMENT AND SELECTION

1 Does the firm achieve a high standard and competitive advantage through recruitment?
2 Is the firm properly aware of its reliance on human resources?
3 Does it, in practice, allocate sufficient time and money to the recruitment process?
4 Is recruitment planned?
5 Is the responsibility for recruitment clearly allocated to a person with proven ability?
6 Has the person responsible undergone any training?
7 What is the record of staff leaving after a short period of employment?
8 Does the firm habitually suffer difficulty in attracting staff, and if so why?
9 Is there any written policy statement on recruitment?
10 Does the firm monitor the achievement of its competitors?
11 To what extent is the firm obliged to compete with government, industry or overseas organisations for its skills?
12 Does the firm plan its manpower needs, and are they derived from overall business plans and related to budgets?
13 What fluctuations of workload have to be provided for, and are they anticipated in time?
14 What are the causes of vacancies?
15 Does the firm suffer financial losses or do clients suffer inconvenience through unfilled vacancies?
16 Are up-to-date and satisfactory job descriptions and job specifications maintained?

17 Are jobs designed to produce reasonable opportunities for satisfaction to the job holder?

18 Is the person to whom each job holder is responsible clearly defined?

19 Do job titles and status align with their responsibility so as to appeal to candidates?

20 Is the recruiting effort adequate in scale?

21 Are all possible sources tapped?

22 Are advertisements well drawn and inserted in the best newspapers or journals?

23 Are useful relationships maintained with local colleges and other relevant training organisations?

24 Are existing staff given adequate opportunities to fill vacancies?

25 Is the person responsible for recruiting properly aware of the attractions of the firm to prospective employees?

26 Are relationships with employment bureaux clear and properly established to provide advice on terms of employment and changes in supply and demand? Is their performance regularly reviewed?

27 Is the cost of recruitment computed, recognised and reasonable?

28 Do the partners properly recognise the influential nature of the selection process on the firm as a whole?

29 Does a policy exist on the quality of staff to be engaged?

30 How is the person responsible for selection chosen; has he demonstrated his ability or undergone any training?

31 Is the interviewer able to judge technical competence?

32 Is the person responsible for supervising the vacant position properly involved in the process?

33 Are the job descriptions and job specifications properly understood by the interviewers?

34 Has the interviewer prepared questions which will reveal the extent to which the candidate meets the requirements of the job?
35 Has the requisite level of technical knowledge been clearly established?
36 Has the level of experience necessary been clearly established?
37 How much training is the firm prepared to give?
38 How can the person's learning level from experience be checked?
39 Is there any danger that candidate's technical knowledge may have become out-of-date?
40 Is there any need for external assistance or advice upon the selection process?
41 Has the firm a good record of satisfaction with employees chosen in the past?
42 What intensity of personal drive or ambition is sought in the candidate, and if found, does the job offer a matching opportunity?
43 Does the work demand a strong sense of vocation in the acceptance of the work itself, unsocial hours or self-denial?
44 What level of self-confidence should the candidate display?
45 Does the job provide a challenge, and what degree of competitive spirit should the job holder possess?
46 Does the work demand empathy with the clients and what questions will test its presence in the candidate?
47 Does the work demand the rapid assimilation of information or interpretation of biased or incomplete information? What level of experience and intelligence is appropriate?
48 Does the activity demand good communication? If so, with whom and at what level?
49 Of the listed talents or characteristics sought, what weight should be attached to each?

50 Will the job holder be the subject of a fidelity bond, and was he informed of this at the first interview? Will the job holder need a current and unendorsed driving licence?
51 Was a reasonable choice left at the end of the first interview?
52 Is an adequate amount of time allowed for each interview and are interruptions avoided?
53 Are adequate opportunities given to candidates to express themselves?
54 Are proper notes kept for future reference?
55 Do the notes comment upon the candidate's bearing, self-confidence, dress, health and quality of speech?
56 Were the features of the job fully and frankly explained?
57 What conclusions may be drawn from the candidate's progress in his basic education?
58 What postgraduate activities illustrate the candidate's development?
59 What conclusions may be drawn from the candidate's career pattern?
60 For what reasons has the candidate changed his past employment?
61 What is the candidate seeking in the new post?
62 Can the firm offer the quality of work and opportunity the candidate is seeking?
63 Does the candidate display the qualities and character suitable to represent the firm?
64 Will the candidate's husband or wife contribute to his work?
65 Does the depth of the final selection discussion demonstrate the thoroughness of the procedures?

'Grief never mended no broken bones, and as good people's wery scarce, what I says is, make the most on 'em.'

Charles Dickens

CHAPTER 6

Personnel management

The advantages gained in personnel selection need to be maintained and further developed in the subsequent relationship. Staff cannot be taken for granted. This subject of personnel management covers a wide area and includes not only the legal aspects of employment, but the induction of new staff, training, discipline, motivation by salary and other benefits, promotion and finally the termination of the contract. All managers must therefore acquire adequate knowledge and skill in the subject both to avoid penalties under statute law and to release the full potential of people for whom they are responsible. This applies to the partners, the personnel manager and all those who are able to engage, discipline, supervise or dismiss people to the extent required by their position.

In this chapter, some of the legal obligations that arise will be reviewed and then those activities which, when well performed, distinguish the progressive and happy firms from those largely inhabited by time servers.

Employment

Under *The Employment Protection (Consolidation) Act, 1978*, any person employed for more than sixteen hours per week must be given a written statement setting out the names of the parties to the contract, the date that employment commenced, the pay and method of its calculation, hours of work, holiday entitlement and holiday pay, arrangements during sickness, the job title and notice of termination to be given and received. As it is permissible to refer to standard documents, it may be advisable to prepare a set contract which can also define:

1 The right of the employer to change the terms of the contract.
2 The rights of the parties in relation to patents, which can be very important when research is undertaken.
3 Restrictions on former employees undertaking work for clients of the firm, i.e. touting instructions after leaving.
4 Any special rules of the profession or firm.

Under the Act all changes have to be notified in writing, and procedures for the handling of grievances are set out, as is also the method of computing the period of employment. Special conditions apply to part-time employees, often found in the professions. The Act also stipulates the minimum period of notice, which increases with length of service, up to twelve weeks after twelve years, and the minimum pay during the period of notice whether the employee is working or not. The Act covers breaches of contract that might occur during the period of notice, which can be a time of bad will.

Redundancy, a common and perhaps a permanent feature of business, is dealt with by *The Employment Protection Act, 1975*, and *The Employment Protection (Consolidation) Act, 1978*. It occurs when a job disappears upon the closure, contraction or reorganisation of a business. The word redundancy is not a euphemism for dismissal, which occurs where a person is dismissed for inefficiency, unsuitability, bad conduct or ill-health. Procedures are laid down and must be followed. They stipulate, amongst other things, that an employer proposing to dismiss fewer than ten people must give fourteen days' advance notice to the Department of Employment of intention to claim the rebates which are available, and that if more than ten employees are to be dismissed sixty days' notice may be required. Fines and penalties are included for non-compliance. An employee may be entitled to redundancy payment after two years' service, and the Act applies to the dismissal of one person and can include domestic servants. In those professions that suffer periodic recession, for example that of architecture, the Act must be considered in formulating employment policy.

The Sex Discrimination Act, 1976, makes it unlawful to discriminate against either a man or a woman on the grounds of sex or marital status in recruitment, terms, conditions or training. It also extends to benefits and promotion. The Act applies to any employer of more than five persons in one or a number of separate establishments. Discrimination can occur if an employer treats an employee, on the grounds of the employee's sex, less favourably than he would treat a man in similar circumstances. This extends to the recruitment and engagement of staff or in deciding who may be invited to apply. Advertisements must not indicate any intention to discriminate, e.g. the use of such a word as 'waiter'. Certain tightly drawn exceptions exist where there is a genuine occupational need for a person of a particular sex or where the nature of the establishment justifies that selection. Employment agencies are the subject of special clauses, and being engaged full-time in that work requires additional knowledge. Of importance to the professions is the fact that it is unlawful in a firm of six or more partners to discriminate in taking in a new partner. Victimisation can occur and is provided for in the Act, as are the procedures for complaints and enforcement.

Under *The Disabled Persons (Employment) Acts, 1944* and *1958*, employers of more than twenty people have an obligation to employ a percentage of registered disabled persons, and the Acts and Regulations require the maintenance of specified records.

The insurance of employees is compulsory for any employer, and a Certificate of Insurance must be displayed at the employer's premises and anywhere his employees are at work. The amount of cover required as of 1979 is £2,000,000 for any one incident involving any one employee. Professions are included and an employer includes a self-employed person. These requirements are set out in *The Employers' Liability (Compulsory Insurance) Act, 1969, The Employers' Liability (Compulsory Insurance) General Regulations Act, 1971*, and *The Employers' Liability (Defective Equipment) Act, 1969.*

Equality between the sexes under the Sex Discrimination Act is also a matter for which there is legislation under *The Equal Pay Act, 1970*. Designed to eliminate discrimination in matters of pay or terms of contract, it applies to every business, however small. It provides for an equality clause to be implied in contracts of employment and specifies assumptions in job evaluation to prevent circumventing the intention of the Act.

The Employment Protection (Consolidation) Act, 1978, affects every business, even to the extent of a firm employing only one person. It is an Act of which every employer should have some knowledge. Liabilities arise in connection with part-time employees and penalties for breach can be heavy. Broadly it provides for guarantee payments during periods of short-time working, and sets out rules governing dismissal, unfair dismissal and redundancy. The total cost of an unfair dismissal may amount to over £13,000.

The Employment Protection Act, 1975, created the Advisory, Conciliation and Arbitration Service (ACAS), which is concerned to improve industrial relations, extend collective bargaining and generate codes of practice. With the agreement of the parties it may refer disputes to the Central Arbitration Committee.

The industrial tribunals hear complaints brought before them by employees and unions. They may require documents and evidence to be submitted to them. Conciliation officers are charged with the duty of promoting settlements. Wage councils have powers to fix terms and conditions as well as pay and holiday pay. Trade union recognition, and procedures to achieve it, are laid down, and where conciliation fails, the Central Arbitration Committee may order an employee to comply with the terms it specifies.

Where an employer suspends an employee on medical grounds, the employer may be liable to continue the latter's pay for up to twenty-six weeks. Furthermore, unless he informs a replacement of the temporary nature of the work when engaging him, he could be guilty of an unfair dismissal when the original person returns to take up his duties.

Where a woman becomes pregnant she may be entitled, in a stipulated circumstance, to maternity pay and the right to return to her work afterwards. Dismissal because of pregnancy can constitute an unfair dismissal and the terms of her re-engagement must not place her at a disadvantage. Maternity pay may be reclaimed from the Maternity Pay Fund to the full amount. However, a woman who is employed by her husband is not entitled to these benefits.

The Act makes it unlawful for an employer to take any action against an employee for the purpose of preventing him from becoming a member of a trade union or from taking part in the activities of a union. It requires the employer to permit the employee, by the grant of time off, to participate in union activities which, under certain conditions, may be on the employer's premises. It permits an employee to take time off for public duties. This is limited to justices of the peace, local authorities, members of statutory tribunals, certain regional authorities, local authority educational establishments and water authorities.

A person who has been employed for more than twenty-six weeks is entitled to ask for a written statement of the reasons for dismissal, which statement may be admissible evidence at subsequent proceedings. If the employee makes a complaint of unfair dismissal which is accepted by the tribunal, it may make an order for the re-instatement of the employee. Further it may specify sums payable by the employer, including arrears, to place the employee where he would have been but for the dismissal. A successor to a business may be bound by a re-engagement order in respect of an employee dismissed by his predecessor. Alternatively an order for compensation may be made. There are provisions for basic awards and additional awards. The practitioner in any doubt about the proposed dismissal of a member of his staff, or the staff of a practice that he contemplates purchasing, should consider the employees carefully and seek advice if he feels that he is taking a risk. Similarly the continued employment of staff members who are of doubtful value should not be considered if, through feelings of kindness, potential liabilities may be greatly increased.

The professional who is engaged in the retail trade, e.g. the pharmacist, will require some knowledge of *The Shops Act, 1950*, the object of which is to protect shop assistants from excessive working hours. It also stipulates the maximum working period without a rest interval, meal times, weekly holidays and half holidays. It places a limitation upon Sunday employment, requires the maintenance of records and lays down penalties for infringement.

Discrimination is again the subject of legislation by *The Race Relations Act, 1976*. This Act makes it unlawful, in respect of employment, to discriminate on the grounds of colour, race, nationality, ethnic or national origins. It has been the subject of considerable coverage in the media and much public debate. The Act defines discrimination and discriminatory practices, and as many professions now include large numbers of staff with overseas origins, it should be studied with care. For partners it is necessary to remember that it is unlawful to discriminate against a person when taking a new partner in a similar manner to that set down in the matter of sex discrimination.

Health and safety

The Factories Act may affect a professional person because his activities render his premises 'a factory' for the purposes of the Act, or he may be involved, as part of his work, because of the activities of his clients. The vet may be concerned with the confinement of animals awaiting slaughter, the architect in matters of safety on a building site or the engineer in the repair of locomotives. The Act requires people engaging in designated activities to serve notice of occupation on the District Inspector and to exhibit notices on their premises. Prescribed registers must be kept including particulars of young persons, every accident and every case of industrial disease. The Act also lays down matters concerning the accommodation of clothing, the cleanliness of floors, stairs and passages, ventilation and decoration, washing and toilet facilities and the temperatures to be maintained. Special hazards associated with such things as compressed gases, lifting tackle, cranes, fumes, dangerous substances, boilers, automatic machines and power transmission are the subject of special clauses. The minimum first-aid requirements are similarly set out.

The Offices, Shops and Railway Premises Act, 1963, is of more direct concern to most professional people. The Act defines those activities which when carried on render the premises used 'an office' or 'a shop'. In a similar manner to the Factories Act it provides for minimum standards and facilities for a healthy working environment. Space, lighting, temperature, ventilation and cleanliness are all included, as are washing and toilet facilities, the fencing of machinery, first aid, hoists and lifts and the notification of accidents.

The Factories Act and the Offices, Shops and Railway Premises Act are further extended by *The Health and Safety at Work etc. Act, 1974*. It provides that every employer has a duty to secure healthy and safe conditions for the welfare of the employees. It goes beyond the provision of suitable premises and equipment and extends to the training of personnel. It also makes it a duty for every employee while at work to take reasonable care for his safety and the safety of others and prohibits interference with or vandalism of safety equipment. Inspectors have a right of entry to premises and have wide-ranging powers for the collection of evidence. If they form the opinion that an improvement is necessary, they may issue a notice to that effect.

The busy practitioner may naturally resent the volume and complexity of legislation. Meeting his clients' demands may require working long and irregular hours with short holidays. The few quiet hours available are often insufficient to keep abreast with the technical advances in his calling. Apparently non-productive reading and paperwork diminish that sense of vocation which drives most professionals along. It is not much consolation to reflect that these trends are not likely to diminish, for they are more likely to increase. As complaint is of little value, what constructive reactions are appropriate?

1 The individual practitioner must recognise that dealing with these matters is an integral part of his work and not an additional burden. The non-professional functions must become a routine part of management and their cost allowed for in calculating fees and budgeting for the practice.
2 The quality and status of those responsible for the administrative functions within the firm must increase.

The 'bookkeeper who deals with forms' will become increasingly inadequate.

3 The members of professional bodies must contribute more active support for their organisations in the generation of opinions and ultimate policy to ensure a representative and authoritative common voice and more vigorous lobby.

It is now possible to turn to those aspects of personnel management that are of concern to the manager because they influence the output and enjoyment of the people for whom he is responsible.

Induction

The aim in this phase is to make new employees feel at ease and to become productive as quickly as possible. As to the firm as a whole, they need to be informed of its range of activities and organisations, of their precise terms of employment, working hours and rules of punctuality, first aid and sickness arrangements, whom they should approach with any grievances, and the rule on such matters as time off, private telephone calls, etc. This process of welcome and instruction should be done by a responsible person. A small handbook or printed document saves time and ensures that all items are covered, but cannot replace a personal welcome at a senior level.

The second aspect of induction concerns the work itself and will usually fall to the manager of the department or immediate supervisor. The person must understand to whom he is immediately responsible, the person to whom he will mainly refer for instruction and guidance and the precise nature of the job to be done. Every firm or group develops individual ways for executing routine work, and these special 'rules' or procedures will need explanation. Safety regulations, especially in such places as laboratories, should not be taken for granted or assumed to be matters of common knowledge. In the case of larger firms that may have established and individual procedures for handling clients and their affairs, a manual can be a most valuable and time-saving internal management guide.

Discipline

Breaches of discipline occur in the best-regulated firms. Of importance to the manager is that it is handled consistently and fairly. There must be an understanding of what is permissible and what is not. Most professions are governed by a code of conduct which the qualified should be able to apply without too much difficulty. However, the rigour with which a firm interprets these rules may vary, and guidance will be needed for new and particularly younger staff. In addition to the codes of conduct that govern the profession as a whole, there may be 'house' rules to be explained along with any other helpful tips about the eccentricities of senior partners.

Some professional codes of conduct place an obligation upon their members to ensure that their staff observe certain rules of behaviour, particularly in such matters as supplanting other practitioners and 'touting' for business. The firm's interpretation of these sometimes loosely worded guidelines will also require explanation.

Salary administration

The subject of salary administration is the core of successful personnel management and demands the close attention of the partner responsible for staff and the concern of the partners as a whole. Its detail extends beyond our scope here*

To recruit and retain staff a firm must maintain competitive levels of reward; to motivate staff the incentives must include additional remuneration for higher performance and responsibility. An individual's sense of vocation is not a rational justification for parsimony. Nor should the reluctance of some professional employees to engage in the aggressive bargaining techniques of industry be regarded as a permanent feature or an excuse for procrastination in salary review by the employers of professional people.

To arrive at logical and equitable salary levels, the partners or employers must consider:

*For further reference, see McBeath and Rands, *Salary Administration*, Business Books.

1 The situation in the market place from which they recruit staff. In particular:
   a The level of supply and demand.
   b The salary levels in other areas where people of the skill they require can find alternative employment, e.g. nationalised industry, local government, overseas posts.
   c The salaries being paid by competitors with similar firms.

2 The extent to which their overall objectives and the nature of the work indicates staff above, equal to, or below average calibre. It may be a case of keeping one step ahead of competitors rather than one step behind.

3 The extent to which actual salaries feature in the total benefits of employment, including the fringe benefits now encouraged by taxation, such as:
   a Free or subsidised life assurance and medical insurance.
   b Bonuses to which there is no legal entitlement.
   c Commissions or productivity payments to which the employee is entitled.
   d The provision of a car or car allowance.
   e The strictness with which expenses are defined.
   f Paid leave for postgraduate studies.
   g Pension arrangements.
   h Special rate mortgages.

4 The frequency of review and the realism of calculations to adjust for inflation in living costs.

5 The level and trend of fees that the market will bear and the terms expressed in equivalent salaries.

Having formed an overall policy based on these general external and internal factors, the reward for individual jobs can be considered. These must recognise:

1 That each job should be considered for its profitability in terms of work executed and its value to the organisation of the firm.

2 That the jobs will be assessed in broad grades or bands so that people doing similar jobs with varying levels of ability may be rewarded accordingly. This produces the necessary flexibility within grades and, where the bands

overlap, ensures that the top level of one grade may be paid more than the bottom level in the grade above. Thus a person may advance both within the grade and by promotion to the next grade.

3 That the salary range of a grade may well be larger the more senior the level. Thus a junior clerical worker or laboratory assistant may progress through a narrow band, perhaps related to age, whereas a mature manager or partner may be rewarded over a wide band. In some cases a premium may be paid for exceptional performance.

4 The skill, experience and calibre that the job holder must bring to his work.

In order to ensure that jobs within an organisation bear the correct relationship to one another in salary terms, the grades or bands should be of approximately equal seniority and if ranged 'in rank' of importance should still be in a sensible order. There are sophisticated techniques of job evaluation and classification involving points ratings for such features as skill and responsibility which can be useful for the larger organisation, particularly where jobs are highly diverse in their content.*

This brief review shows that *ad hoc* negotiations with individuals, possibly prompted by a hint of discontent or threat to leave, deprives management of initiative in the core area of a labour-intensive activity. Salary policy must therefore receive the priority and depth of consideration it merits if the firm is to succeed in other areas of personnel management.

Training

Training is essential and costly. The layman is entitled to expect up-to-date advice, and there are very few activities in which the practitioner does not rapidly become out-of-date. The client or patient is equally entitled to competence, which implies the need for training in the application of professional skill as new techniques become available. The public is entitled

*For more, see M. Armstrong, *Management Practice*, Kogan Page.

to value, and this demands training in managing the professional's resources.

Because of its cost and importance a training programme must be systematic in order to obtain maximum return on expenditure. Furthermore management must provide an incentive for people to train so that there is real effort to climb the ladder and not just a helping hand. Training should be designed to meet the real and foreseen operational needs of the firm and its job holders in terms of results and standards.

The process must start with an analysis of the job descriptions and specifications and, by comparison with the performance of those holding them, a definition of the areas where improvement is needed. At middle and senior levels, training of this type must be tailored to each case and based on observation of performance. At junior levels general training will be more appropriate. In addition to the training of the individual, which may vary greatly, general progress in the discipline will involve the firm in general courses. Thus the person responsible for training will be considering the development of each individual and the need of the firm as a whole to keep up-to-date. Because pressures of current work tend to take priority, a programme will usually be necessary, supervised from a senior level, to maintain momentum.

In considering the training activities the partners must naturally start with a calculation of a budget that they can afford. Then, within these means, they must identify those members of their staff who will require training to fulfil the roles that it is hoped they will fulfil in one, five and even ten years. Research will usually reveal a surprisingly large number of low-cost facilities available.

Types of training

The type of training facilities will depend largely on the size of the organisation and the budget. They include:

1 Special 'in house' courses. These may be designed by, or in collaboration with, consultants specialising in this type of work. They are relatively expensive but may produce a more economic answer if the course can be repeated a

sufficient number of times or, at least in part, recorded. In so far as the special or confidential techniques of a firm are concerned, they may be a necessary part of a mixed 'in house' and external programme.

2 Courses run by professional institutions governing the discipline in question.
3 Local technical colleges and university vacation courses.
4 Correspondence courses.
5 Programmed private study subject to supervision of a senior or appropriate member of staff.

To provide a proper incentive for training, the advance of salaries within a grade (and promotion) should be related to a person's performance in the training programme.

Welfare

A general policy is desirable to cover a number of additional contingencies if staff are to feel they are handled with fairness and consistency. These include:

1 Death, prolonged sickness or permanently reduced ability.
2 Assistance in the case of family difficulty.
3 Convictions for offences that touch on a person's reputation or ability to perform his work, e.g. loss of driving licence, theft, etc.
4 Periodic medical examinations and action to be taken in such cases as high blood pressure, obesity, heart disease, ulcers and alcoholism.
5 The partners and managers should maintain a watchful eye on the health and morale of their staff and hopefully detect problems in the early stages, before they become a serious difficulty to the individual or a loss to the practice.

Summary

The law which regulates and affects the relations between employer and employee has been of interest to the State for centuries, as testified by the medieval Statute of Labourers.

Further, this interest has been expressed by an increasing number of statutes in each century as the scale and complexity of employment has increased. Similarly the body of case law has clarified the contractual relationship over the years. But it is in the last two decades that Parliament has chosen to regulate nearly every aspect of employment to an extent that it is now commercially dangerous to proceed in ignorance of the law. And it is a law that is continually changing. The modern employer is therefore obliged to ensure that personnel are managed in accordance with current law. This is a management responsibility of growing importance and one which demands the allocation of appropriate time and effort if the risk of serious difficulty is to be avoided.

However, the demands made of enlightened management extend far further than mere law and regulation. They in themselves can only produce a sterile relationship in which the parties know, or think they know, where they stand. Professional practice is usually a labour-intensive activity and therefore one which relies on the quality of the relationships between all concerned. There are matters that cannot be taken for granted and for which responsibility must be clearly assigned. The advantages that can be gained by the good selection of staff are only available to those who consolidate their investment by maintaining high standards of personnel administration.

This work begins with the induction and training of the new employee, a period when first and important impressions are made. It continues in the form of consistent guidance, discipline, training and motivation. The work embraces salary administration and the careful selection of other rewards, further training in the discipline itself and management training where these responsibilities occur. The conduct of training programmes requires careful planning if their cost is to yield the maximum benefit to the firm and the individual. Finally it includes all aspects of personnel welfare, not only in the provision of amenities but in matters of health and action on those occasions of misfortune that can occur to us all.

The entire success of personnel management starts with a proper recognition at partnership and management level of what one may call the 'new era' of employment. An age has been entered where the cost and consequences of employment are such that manpower cannot be squandered; where sub-standard performance cannot be tolerated; where change must be seen as opportunity and not decay, and in which people rank with, and must be rewarded according to, their useful productivity.

Checklist – Chapter 6

PERSONNEL MANAGEMENT

1 Is the importance attached to personnel management consistent with that accorded to personnel selection?
2 Is responsibility for personnel management clearly assigned at partnership level and satisfactorily delegated where necessary?
3 Has the person responsible for personnel undergone any training for the work?
4 Does the firm properly understand its legal duties and obligations?
5 Are all contracts of employment satisfactory and in order, and have changes been made where necessary?
6 Would the firm benefit from the adoption of its own contract of employment?
7 Has the firm suffered from an unacceptable level of disputes on matters of employment?
8 Have the full implications of redundancies been appreciated?
9 Does the firm satisfactorily avoid discrimination?
10 Does the firm comply with the Factories Acts, The Offices, Shops and Railway Premises Act and other current legislation in all respects?
11 Is electrical and mechanical office and laboratory equipment checked, as a matter of routine, at regular intervals, and is responsibility for safety clearly assigned?
12 Have the quality and status of the person responsible for administrative functions kept abreast of the demands upon them?
13 Is there any risk that lax discipline or supervision can expose staff or clients to danger or un-

necessary risk? Do actual practices vary from safe practices through over-familiarity with dangerous work or substances?

14 Has the induction process for new staff been planned to ensure that new staff are quickly put at ease and can make an early contribution?

15 Is there a formal document to acquaint new staff with the activities of the organisation, details of their work and the firm's 'house rules'?

16 Are matters of discipline handled fairly, consistently and at the right level?

17 Has the firm created a policy for salary administration and how frequently is it reviewed?

18 Has a comparative study been made of the terms offered by competitors?

19 Does the firm retain the initiative in salary reviews?

20 Has consideration been given to the full range of benefits that can be offered to staff?

21 Is each job valued according to its contribution to profitability and the organisation as a whole?

22 Are the salary 'bands' sufficiently wide to reward differing levels of experience and ability within each grade?

23 Is training the subject of formal consideration and programming? Is there a training budget?

24 Are discussions held at regular intervals with each member of the staff to review his progress, current ambitions and training needs?

25 Is training systematic and based on an adequate knowledge of available courses?

26 Do job descriptions and specifications include information on necessary training for the job holder?

27 Are welfare matters the subject of an agreed policy?

28 When staff leave are their reasons acceptable or do they indicate a need for improvement?

29 How often is the subject of staff calibre, morale and motivation reviewed by management?

30 What does the firm offer that makes it a more desirable employer than its competitors?

31 Is the firm exposed to any risk of key personnel leaving and setting up in competition or inducing other valued staff to leave?

32 What level of pride and confidence do the partners display in their staff?

33 What level of pride and confidence do the staff display in their partners?

'I know you believe you understand what you think I said. But I am not sure that you realise that what you heard is not what I meant.'

Anon

CHAPTER 7

Communications

Sadly, the ability to communicate is often underdeveloped because most people believe that they were born with it. As one approaches this subject it must be recognised that it is an activity in which major improvement is needed. As Thomas L. Martin Jr wrote, 'The inevitable result of improved and enlarged communication between different levels in a hierarchy is a vastly increased area of misunderstanding.'* It is surprising to find such low standards of communication commonly accepted without comment in the business world. Business activity is analagous to communication itself because it is both purposeful and interactive. If one peels away the walls of an office block, the majority of the people exposed will be engaged in it. They will be revealed interviewing, attending meetings, speaking on the telephone, dictating and reading letters. They will be persuading, enquiring, instructing, agreeing and arguing. The basic business activities of researching a market, evolving a new product, formulating policy, procuring finance, selling and organising resources all involve an oral and written flow of ideas. The basic business activities of forming a contract — the offer, the counter-offer and acceptance — which are the very heartbeat of commercial activity, are all acts of communicating.

*From J.G. Dunne, *Malice in Blunderland* , McGraw-Hill.

A manager, in organising, controlling and reviewing the activities of others, relies upon his capability to transmit and receive information efficiently. The professional person's activities of taking a client's instructions, diagnosis, explanation, instruction, prognosis and persuasion are similarly influenced by the accuracy of his comprehension and expression.

Communication permits organisation

The community of a company or firm operates by the continual exchange of information among the people that form it. Its efficiency therefore depends on the success with which the efforts of many, perhaps numbering thousands, can be directed, motivated and controlled. Business, and this includes the professional world, relies on delegation. Few professionals can manage without the assistance of secretarial or technical people.

Delegation, upon which nearly all commercial and professional activity relies, is impossible without effective communication. This in itself would be sufficient to justify the importance of the subject and merit greater emphasis upon it in education and training, but in fact it goes even further. The large business organisation, essential to the modern economy in many industries, can only survive if its control is decentralised. Delegation within a business unit in one location often proves a stumbling block for management. How much more intractable the matter becomes when numbers of branches or even overseas units are involved. If one cannot achieve an intelligent dialogue between the controlling centre and the subordinate parts, there is little hope for success. The alternative is a central bureaucratic control which in a very short period will demonstrate a lack of competitive capability. In short, both delegation and decentralisation, essential to the modern economy, depend largely on the coordination of the whole by the nervous system of communications.

Communications in the commercial and professional world

In many ways a professional activity can be compared to a typical commercial company.

1 The market place Successful business operators are frequently characterised by the close contact they keep with their competitors and the market place in which they operate. There is a continuous flow of information about customers' needs, and while present efforts are directed towards meeting them, future activities are planned to anticipate them.

The marketing activity is the spearhead. If it loses contact with the future needs of the market place, the company is in serious danger and may one day be confronted with the potentially fatal situation of obsolescent products or irrelevant services. In short the company must be in constant and intelligent communication with its customers. Similarly a profession that fails to keep in contact with the real and developing needs of its clients must, sooner or later, find its relevance challenged. It may be by the emergence of a competing professional body, by some challenge in parliament of its privileged position, or by a process in which its best talents drift away. At the level of the individual firm it may be by a diminishing share of the available work in the community, as new clients are recommended elsewhere and old clients die out. The process of contact with the customer is obviously one of intelligent communication.

2 Sources of finance Finance is a commercial resource as necessary as manpower, materials or energy. But it is a resource for which there is a great deal of competition, and the supply never equals the demand. Proven performance or 'track record' needs to be presented in such a way that professional lenders or investors will provide the necessary finance for operating and expanding the undertaking. Ineptitude in this will continually thwart progressive management; consequently the standards of communication between a company and the providers of its finance are as important as those that it maintains with its customers and staff. In the professional world this aspect may be of less significance, particularly if the practitioner is expressly prevented by his professional code of conduct from joint ventures with unqualified people. He will nevertheless be foolish if he fails to maintain good relations with his bank manager, and these are best built by keeping him well informed.

3 The government It is fashionable to complain about government performance in handling industry and the professions. Sometimes the complaint is of excessive intervention; on other occasions it is for failure to take action. Whatever the rights and wrongs are of a particular issue, one frequent and serious allegation is that of lack of consultation with interested parties. Whether it is the arrogance of autocracy or the clumsiness of bureaucracy matters little if the profession is guilty of failing to put its case or views effectively. As the proper spokesman for the silent membership, a professional body has a responsibility to project the opinions of its members to government.

4 Communication with employees The price paid for bad labour relations has been demonstrated by those industries plagued with them. Fortunately the professions have been relatively free of this problem so far. As skilled and intelligent people, professionals require, and are entitled to expect, high standards of personnel management and a sensible dialogue with management. Failure to maintain a feeling of vocation and adequate job satisfaction, which are matters of great importance to professional people, will result in the best talent drifting out of the particular activity. In industry a failure to consult has often been the trigger of labour difficulties. One investigator makes the figurative point that 'communication between management and workers is filtered by a funnel with the large end facing upwards. The workers must get their thoughts up through the small end of the funnel.'* If the professions are to avoid the problems of some industries, it is necessary for management to be articulate in its demands, both for itself as managers and in its dealings with subordinates and provoke an upward as well as a downward flow of

*V. Packard, *The Status Seekers*, p 129, Penguin.

information. Of Marks and Spencer, Anthony Jay has stated: 'Every director and executive and headquarters manager visited at least one store a week to talk to the staff in the front line.'* This is what communications is largely about.

The mechanics of communication

The basic questions that arise have been defined as†:

1 What should be communicated?
3 Who should communicate?
3 When should information be communicated?
4 Where should information be communicated?
5 How should information be communicated?

This instinctive awareness of the needs of others is one of the hallmarks of the good manager. He is immediately able to detect that information coming before him which needs to be passed on. Further, he will instinctively know when it needs interpretation, qualification, simplification or suppression.

Frequently he will receive information in the form of an objective to be achieved. It is then for him to decide on the further delegation of the work, its allocation among his subordinates, the resources that he will require for the assignment, the organisation best suited to the task and the method by which he is going to control the process. As he absorbs the instructions, plans and executes the activity, a series of potential communication errors emerge:

1 He has not properly understood his instructions, either because they were not correctly transmitted or were distorted in the process of transmission by an intermediate handler or were incorrectly understood by the intermediate.
2 An error or omission has occured in his instructions so that distortion takes place in the process of delegation by him.

According to the complexity of the matter, the communications process should start with a check of the input

* A. Jay, *The Corporation Man*, p 195. Pelican.

† Frank Finch in *The Concise Encyclopedia of Management* Technique, p 36, Heinemann.

information. He may not command the necessary resources or have the necessary authority to execute the task. He may feel that the instructions should come from 'higher up'. Similarly he may feel that the person making the request lacks the necessary authority. This can easily occur in loose organisation where people's job specifications and authority are blurred or overlap. It can be very confusing where instructions come from the 'wrong' person and demoralising where they place the recipient in a conflict of loyalties. Even when a person has undoubted authority, such as the managing director or proprietor of a business, resentment and confusion can result where communications fly 'over the heads' of managers. Thus the question of 'who' should communicate is one of real and everyday importance.

The timing of communications can be critical. The catastrophes that have occurred as a result of the late arrival of messages are but extreme examples of everyday occurrences in business. Premature communications can be equally dangerous, especially if they are incomplete through lack of thinking-through by the sender. The timing of communications can be used to impart rhythm into business in the form of regular reports and meetings.

The place chosen for communication can have considerable impact. Some morsels may be more effectively and rapidly spread by a veiled hint at a cocktail party — the grapevine approach — while others will be more telling at a formal announcement. Delicate matters or those that are potentially controversial or painful may have a far better chance of success if the time, the place and the method are selected with care.

To whom to communicate is not always as obvious as it first appears. As a general rule it is usually better to communicate too much than to be parsimonious with information. The harm done by sending a copy of a letter to a colleague 'for information' is invariably less than the risk of leaving him in ignorance. It is not easy to reply to the complaint that starts with the words 'if only I had known'.

Quality of communication

The output from most information systems is only as good as the input. It has been said that if you put rubbish into a computer you get rubbish out of it; the only difference is that it is impressively printed. There is a tendency in many large organisations to confuse the sophistication of their equipment with quality of thought, when in reality it only proves their ability to spend money. *In communications, quality is of the essence*. There are few important matters that are not best dealt with by first making a written draft, even if they are subsequently to be delivered orally and thereafter confirmed in writing. The errors of omission or ambiguity are more easily detected in drafts. A worse offence is committed by those people who use the act of communication as an opportunity to distort information for their own purposes. The natural desire of people to present themselves in the best light can cause them consciously or subconsciously to colour information passing through their hands. Between two people the biased communication can usually be noticed, but when the message passes along a chain it can become progressively distorted until it reaches its destination. It is for each person to watch the honesty with which he handles other people's statements, and for managers to be vigilant about distortion by their staff.

In so far as a manager's subordinates will tend to set their standards from his example, care taken will pay additional dividends. Some young people seem to experience difficulty in acquiring a feel for the subject, and, of course, people who tend to be self-centred can be aggravatingly weak in sensing the needs of others. Some people of curiously secretive disposition can be found in most large organisations hoarding useful information. It requires patience and training to improve matters where standards are low, and this is one of the responsibilities of management.

In the case of a lack of communication, the omission may be readily detected because the silence itself raises a question. Incomplete messages are perhaps more dangerous, especially where the omission is not clear from the content. Where people are working under pressure, it is all too easy for them to send hasty messages via secretaries who may not understand the information they are conveying. It is a good habit to follow up messages with personal contact as soon as possible, and where the subject matter merits it, to confirm them in writing.

When using telex or telegraph some people contrive a language of such economy as to be virtually unintelligible or, worse, to bristle with ambiguity. The use of telex is spreading and is a great convenience. Messages should always be drafted by hand and checked before transmission and the copy double checked. This is especially important if the recipient is abroad and may have difficulty clarifying a message.

Methods of communication

Communications may be categorised in a number of ways. There are the high-speed methods of radio, television, telephone and public address or the slow one of letters (sometimes of unpredictable speed). However, while speed is a significant factor, communications will be considered under the three categories of oral, written and mass media.

1 *Oral:*
   - *a* The interview of or meeting between two or more people.
   - *b* The formal, private meeting, e.g. board meetings and the formal 'open' meeting.
   - *c* The telephone.
   - *d* The lecture.

2 *Written:*
   - *a* Correspondence.
   - *b* Reports.
   - *c* Telex and telegraph.

3 *Mass media:*
   - *a* The notice board.
   - *b* The newspaper, magazine, house journal and news sheet.
   - *c* Films, television, slides, tapes and records.

Oral communications

The interview and meetings Face to face and in private conversation, people generally communicate efficiently. Managers spend a large proportion of their time engaged in conversation and attending meetings, and professionals are similarly involved. The more effectively they can deal with meetings, the more efficient their performance will become. The conduct of the personal interview was discussed when the selection of prospective employees was considered, and most of these points apply equally to business meetings. To a large extent the value of a meeting is determined by the person who plans it and the clarity with which its purpose is understood. Whether it is to consult, to conclude, to review or to issue instructions or announce policy must be clear.

The first question is — 'Is the meeting necessary and is it the best means of achieving the objective?' While a gathering of mutually involved people may be the fastest way of exchanging information, it is not always the best. With some weak managers it can be a subconscious device for the evasion of difficult issues. If the numbers involved are too large, a meeting can be cumbersone and the force of predetermined instructions can be weakened by undesirable debate. Also meetings are not cheap. Skilled time is costly and four people meeting for a morning may cost several hundred pounds in lost earnings. Meetings can also inhibit the flow of information, especially if one or more of those attending is in a defensive or embarrassed position. Meetings are not without certain dangers. The accidental omission to invite a person who may feel excluded can place an assembly in a conspiratorial light, even when this is not the case. Thought concerning who should attend and who should be informed of the event is essential. It is also well to reflect on the background circumstances, purpose and personalities involved before calling a meeting. When first joining or leading a team, it is instructive to observe how meetings are traditionally handled and how people react at them as they provide a good clue to the character of the group.

A clear idea of the objective of a meeting is essential. Broadly speaking, gatherings are usually called either for the exchange of information or for the more executive purpose of declaring policy and issuing instructions. Sometimes the former purpose leads to the latter when 'on the spot' decisions are made. Where the aim is to gather information, the following factors merit attention:

1 Adequate notice must be given to enable those attending to prepare their contributions. This means that the period of notice should be as generous as possible, and the agenda should be settled in advance. Further, any information or reports that members need to study should be circulated in time. It is pointless to expect constructive comment on information sprung at the last minute or, worse, at the meeting itself.

2 Has the person calling the meeting prepared all the information that he will need to contribute? It is difficult to avoid the conclusion after some meetings that they were convened on impulse by a chairman anxious to display his total ignorance of the subject.

3 A free flow of information may be stifled or biased if those attending are of greatly differing seniority, from conflicting profit centres, from functions that compete for limited resources or are otherwise in conflict. It is sometimes a good idea to prepare for a meeting with a private word or two. It is essential to avoid unnecessary open criticism of individuals either present or absent.

4 Where meetings are of a regular nature, it is helpful to remember the words of Anthony Jay*: 'It is all too easy for meetings which start with sound operational objectives to fossilise into ritual assemblies whose only value is to treat cases of social deprivation by regular group therapy.'

5 If visual aid equipment is required, it should be checked to avoid the comedy of failed light bulbs, incorrect plugs and upside-down slides.

6 It is almost certain that records will be needed, and their extent and circulation should be decided in advance. There may be part of the meeting that is best left unrecorded for frank or private discussion.

*A. Jay, *The Corporation Man*, p 218, Pelican.

Where a meeting is called to issue instructions or announce policy, it will probably be of a different tone. The information will tend to flow in one direction, followed by questions and clarified by answers. The following points merit attention:

1 Is a meeting the best means of issuing the instructions? If they are complex or controversial the questions may all too easily lead to confusion or become reactionary. A memorandum may give the subject matter a better chance to 'sink in'. Unpalatable instructions may be more tactfully conveyed at a series of private discussions.
2 An assembly of mixed grades deprives the senior members, for good or ill, of the opportunity to handle the instruction in their own way as they delegate the work for which they will be accountable.
3 Written confirmation of instructions may be required for issue at the meeting to avoid members acting immediately on an oral misunderstanding.
4 How are questions and objections to be dealt with? While the authority or force of the instruction must not be diluted, it is equally important to avoid the subsequent criticism of inflexibility or failure to provide an opportunity for reasonable consultation.
5 What records are to be kept and to whom will they be circulated?

The formal private meeting It is not commonly appreciated that the conduct of formal, private meetings, for example, those of a board of directors, are subject to a body of law. In the case of local authorities and the meetings of members of a company, they may be the subject of statute law. The board meetings of companies or the managing committees of sporting associations, clubs and the like, are also subject to adopted rules in their articles of association. Anyone responsible for convening or conducting meetings should acquaint themselves both with the general law and the particular rules under which they are operating.* Failure to observe correct procedure can invalidate not only a particular resolution but the entire proceedings. Grave consequences can

*T.P.E. Curry and J.R. Sykes, *The Conduct of the Meeting*, Jordan.

flow from too much reliance on common sense or the subsequent discovery, perhaps after contracts have been entered into, that a meeting has been acting *ultra vires* or irregularly. For those professions concerned with company law, these matters will be second nature, and it may fall to them to advise on procedure. However, for others, the involvement may not appear to be so direct but can be equally important, and many a professional adviser has rendered valuable assistance by querying the actions of a meeting that appears to be falling into error.

Time spent familiarising oneself with the basic rules, if not some of the finer points, can enhance the authority of the adviser and give him a considerable advantage if he should become involved in a dispute as a member of a meeting. It has been said of the late Sir Winston Churchill that many of his best points were scored as a result of his mastery of the procedure of the House of Commons.

It is beyond the scope of this book to examine the legal aspects of the conduct of meetings, and the following observations are drawn mainly to illustrate the way in which procedural matters influence the efficiency of the communication process.

Convening meetings Regulations normally prescribe the way in which meetings are to be convened and who is entitled to attend them. Any director may convene a board meeting, though it is customarily arranged by the secretary on the instructions of the chairman. Failure to give the stipulated notice, or reasonable notice if none is laid down, can invalidate the meeting. It will be noticed already that one of the prime considerations is the avoidance of unfair dealing with a minority and that the aim is to be fair, reasonable and open. There can be no 'trickiness' in these matters. For the same underlying reason, the notice should give an accurate picture of the matters to be discussed in order that a member can properly decide whether or not he wishes to attend and prepare any contribution that he may want to make. The chairman, in conducting the business, should confine matters to those on the agenda, or he will run the risk of subsequent complaint by an absentee who would have attended had he known the true content of the meeting. This could invalidate proceedings, and for that reason it is improper to deal with important matters under such comprehensive titles as 'any other business', which should be reserved for small administrative matters that arise.

Procedure Again it is necessary to ensure that there is strict adherence to any stipulated procedure. Generally the first matter is the appointment of a chairman who may be elected or sometimes nominated. The quality of a chairman is crucial. Unfortunately many small organisations, particularly those of a charitable nature, often persuade people of standing rather than talent to take the office, with the result that proceedings suffer. 'The ideal chairman should be a man of infinite tact and patience, possess a judicial mind, be able to command the respect of the meeting, be absolutely impartial in his rulings — never allowing the latter to be questioned.'* His duties demand familiarity with the statutory rules, standing orders or regulations of the body over which he is presiding, for he must ensure that:

1 The meeting was properly convened.
2 The procedures laid down are followed.
3 The agenda is adhered to.
4 All people present have a proper opportunity to speak.
5 The proceedings are orderly.
6 Proper records are kept.

These characteristics imply an appointment of a well respected person.

Each speech should be addressed to the chair, and the speaker should adhere to the motion or subject under discussion, keep within a time limit if one is set and at all times be as brief as possible. A second speech is not normally permissible at a formal meeting unless a proposer is using the customary right of reply. It is for the chairman to decide in what order the speakers should contribute and to be scrupulously fair in allocating opportunities to those present to air their views.

*T.P.E. Curry and J.R. Sykes, *The Conduct of the Meeting*, p 18, Jordan.

Motions A motion is merely a proposal, which should be clear and concise, sometimes written, and remains a motion until it is resolved when it becomes a resolution and should be recorded.

Amendments Amendments can be a source of difficulty. They should be dealt with in logical order and allowed whenever there is doubt, as failure to allow an amendment to be moved may invalidate a resolution. However, this can call for fine judgement by the chairman, for equally an amendment should not take the meeting outside the scope of its purpose.

Minutes Minutes are often allowed to contain far too much information. While their accuracy is paramount, they should only record resolutions and decisions and not an extended account of the debate. It is sensible if they record the arrival and departure of members of board or committee during the proceedings, so that there can be no subsequent doubt regarding who was present at a particular stage. The exact wording of resolutions should be used and instructions given should be carefully recorded. The minute book should be indexed for convenient reference at subsequent meetings. The chairman should sign the minutes when they are approved as correct, which is often the first or second formality at the next meeting.

Documentation for meetings It will be appreciated from the foregoing comments on procedure how necessary it is to ensure that each person is given a proper opportunity both to influence the work and share the responsibility of the body of which he is a member. Whether he attends because he is a shareholder or has been elected, his rights must be observed. One can see the emphasis on communication in the obligation to ensure that every person who is entitled to attend is given ample opportunity to do so. This theme occurs again in confining the meeting to matters announced in advance and in the handling of motions and amendments.

But the most scrupulously conducted meeting can still make the most disastrous errors of judgement, and even lose control of the activities for which it is responsible, if the board papers and reports are not handled well. To monitor progress and control effectively — that is to say, in time to make corrective decisions or allowances — management must receive the right information about the right things at the right time. A company secretary can make a considerable contribution in arranging for this to occur. If the board is to function as it should — and the following comments apply equally to many managers, particularly in the control of meetings — the handling of papers, i.e. minutes and agendas, is a very important matter. In particular:

1 Minutes and agendas should be circulated in adequate time for all directors to digest their content and form an opinion or frame their questions before the board meeting. Directors may choose to give notice of questions in order that answers may be prepared without the delay of waiting for the next meeting.

2 Minutes and agendas should be presented to the board in such a form that the information can be readily assimilated, particularly by non-executive or part-time directors. In achieving this the following points may be useful:

   a Voluminous information should be avoided or noted in appendices. This will add clarity to the body of the report.

   b The method of presenting regular information should be consistent and wherever possible variances or comparisons should be expressed in percentage terms. This will enable directors more easily to make comparisons and detect trends that may concern them.

   c Information of significance should be accorded the proper priority, and embarrassing or difficult facts should not be buried in the report.

   d The routine reports of subsidiary company managing directors, divisional directors, executives and others should follow a standard pattern and include obligatory headings. Their content should not be left to their discretion. Where reports are left to individuals they may accidently neglect to report such matters as major contract difficulties or overspends or even be tempted to deliberately conceal or delay the reporting of embarrassing information.

e It may be undesirable, and place an unfair burden on the chief executive, if the reports of subsidiary directors and managers are first considered by him at a preliminary chief executive's meeting.

f Reports should have a reasonable blend of narrative and statistics so that directors may obtain an accurate and fair view of the matters before the board.

g There should be an adopted timetable for the reporting of matters that do not require consideration at every meeting, i.e. the utilisation of real estate, insurance, public relations, etc., and this timetable should be adhered to.

h Information should be up-to-date. Response to the early symptoms of difficulty is impossible if the board is provided with only near-historical information.

The type and frequency of reports will vary from time to time, and their contents, relevance and accuracy should be regularly reviewed. However, care should be taken in designing any change to the reporting system that will destroy useful comparisons or cause the directors to lose their feel of the progress of the business. Changes that lead to an improvement in the company's apparent financial position are particularly suspect if they should be motivated by impending or actual cash difficulties. Similarly deep thought should be given to any changes in accounting principles if it is the company's intention to raise money on the basis of the new figures.*

The telephone Had the telephone been invented a few hundred years earlier, an etiquette might have evolved for its use. It is an instrument that requires self-discipline if it is to be used to its best advantage and not as an instrument of torture for friends and business colleagues. Every time that a telephone rings, and this probably numbers several million times a day across the country, someone is interrupted. It is an

*For more, see M. Allsopp, *Survival in Business*, Business Books.

undoubted convenience and an economic method of communication provided that the parties remember that brevity is the keyword, and to this end the following hints are worth remembering:

1 Plan the call. Check that the right person to discuss the matter in hand is the one telephoned, and if possible the alternative person in case he is not available. Make a list of the points to discuss. This is important when telephoning someone with whom one is in regular contact as it can greatly reduce the number of calls. Gather all the information together. The cost and inconvenience of calls is greatly increased by those people who interrupt their conversations while they search around for missing papers to refer to.
2 Upon obtaining a connection state the name and company of the caller and the person required. When on long-distance calls, if the person is not immediately available, ring again rather than hang on. If the person called needs to research for an answer then ask them to call back rather than hang on. Avoid enigmatic little messages like 'so-and-so called but tell him that it didn't matter'.
3 If a secretary or telephone switchboard operater is asked to 'get someone on the line', then be available when the connection is made. It is a common error and bad manners to interrupt someone with a telephone call and not to be available to deal with the conversation when the connection is made.

The switchboard operator should be an asset to any organisation. It is not always easy work. The load can vary from inactivity to pressure of the highest order, and an equable and pleasant temperament is needed. The operator handling incoming calls must know the operation of the firm if she is to channel incoming calls to the appropriate person. Many firms miss a golden opportunity to impress their clients; their miserably low standards have the opposite effect. Callers are left dangling on the telephone without explanation, or treated as if they are of secondary importance to the people within the firm with whom the operator appears to be preoccupied. The operator often gives the first impression of a firm to the caller who may be about to become a client.

Written communications

Correspondence The Post Office is the largest organisation in the United Kingdom. In the year 1977-8 it made a profit exceeding one million pounds per day. This is some indication of the volume of communication that it handles on behalf of industry and commerce.

The bulk of formal communication is by the exchange of letters. Countless millions of contracts are created in this way each year, and it therefore rates as an important business activity. The correspondence file probably represents the only comprehensive, legal record of the progress of a matter. Yet it remains an activity that is largely taken for granted and neglected in education. Many competent practitioners pay little attention to the development of their skills in correspondence, and this is revealed each time one reads their letters or glimpses their badly kept letter files. Perhaps the increased volume of correspondence has debased the coinage. Perhaps, too, the interposed and uninvolved shorthand writer or dictation machine has dulled the essentially personal nature of a letter.

For many, the letter represents an opportunity to impress a client with the orderliness of thinking and the concern with which the firm is undertaking his instructions. In those professions that do not permit advertising, the quality of the notepaper and the printing can reveal good taste and reinforce the identity of the firm in the client's mind. The letter often has legal significance. In the case of a partnership or individual trading without the benefit of limited liability, there is a personal liability for any negligence by the employee, and in most cases the plaintiff will rely, for evidence, on the correspondence from that employee.

For these reasons the partners of a firm should take a keen

interest in the outgoing correspondence if they do not in fact sign every letter. Some firms maintain a central library in which all outgoing letters are filed in chronological order. This system has the following advantages. Firstly, partners can scan or study letters without holding up their posting or filing; secondly, a file can be largely re-created if it should accidentally be lost; and, thirdly, it impedes fraud involving the removal or alteration of letters.

Reports Some practitioners may be largely judged by their ability to write. The quality of a report is largely influenced by the clarity of the thinking upon which it is based. Biased, muddled or superficial thinking is more quickly revealed by the written word than by any other means. Any professional who aspires to succeed in a calling where the written word is important must acquire the facility. Most reports record a combination of fact and opinion, and are intended to convey meaning to a layman or at least one not qualified in the same speciality as the writer. The following hints are useful:

1 Reports should be concise, clear and simple, In producing a concise report the aim should be economy of expression without loss of meaning — just long enough for the purpose. Clarity is essential if the reader is not to be worried by ambiguity or doubtful in his interpretation of what is really meant. Simple sentences using the simple words are always best. All quoted facts must be checked, and any reservations or limitations on their accuracy should be stated, as should their source where appropriate.
2 A report should normally stand by itself. It should not make references to unrecorded conversations or letters that are not included. It should be a self-contained document. A report is often passed on to strangers, totally unknown to the writer and without access to other documents.
3 Fact and opinion should not be confused.
4 Appendices or schedules should be used to avoid cluttering the body of the report with excessive supporting information.
5 Write clearly for the typist. Beware of dictating important

reports; fine shades of meaning are usually best worked out in manuscript.

6 Punctuate with care.

7 Avoid slang or colloquial phrases or cliches. Avoid the use of technical terms that are beyond the comprehension of the reader. If a technical term must be used, it should be explained.

8 Read the judgements of the High Court and study them as often as possible. They are models of style and logic and are instructive on the legal aspects of the professions and commerce generally.

9 Severely limit the use of the first person singular.

10 Take care in making notes that will subsequently be used as the basis of a report e.g. a survey. Taking notes badly leads to a report containing flaws or, worse, guesses.

11 Take care to maintain the confidential nature of all reports.

The process can be accelerated if the writer develops a form appropriate to his work. Most reports fit well into the following layout:

a Recite the instructions. This is important. The restatement of the instructions reminds the adviser what he is doing, reduces the possibility of misunderstanding between the parties and may form a legal basis in the case of a dispute or claim that he acted negligently, inadequately or in excess of instructions.

b Recite the facts *(i)* as instructed, *(ii)* as observed and *(iii)* as deduced.

c State the inferences available, the arguments and their merits. Draw upon any past experience or authorities. Elaborate on future events that might flow from the present situation.

d In the conclusion state the opinion finally adopted and the reasons for coming to that conclusion. Clearly state any reservations, qualifications or weaknesses that might be inherent in the final conclusion. Explain any dangers that might attend a particular action that has been recommended. State any legal reservations that attach to the report, for example, that it is not assignable to the benefit, or to be relied upon by unknown persons.

Writing is a highly personal affair. It is worthwhile to experiment with different methods. The following procedure may be helpful:

1 Where a report is a routine matter, for example, a survey or even a judgement, the form will present less of a problem than if it is, say, a technical paper on a completely new subject. In the latter case, the first phase may be considered as one of 'brainstorming'. Assemble all the available information without worrying too much about the order it is in. Write down every idea that comes to mind, however trivial it may appear to be. The object is to let the thoughts flow. Leave plenty of space between each item as ideas will tend to 'run on', and space will be needed to develop them. In a simple matter with which the author is familiar, this process may only take a few minutes or hours. In a serious exploration of a new area, it might take weeks. Where the process is extended, always jot an idea down when it occurs; few of us have memories as good as we think they are, and related thoughts occur in the most unlikely places.

2 The untidy pile of ideas that will accumulate during the 'brain-storming phase' phase may suggest their own natural order. In a controversial or multi-faceted subject, the important thing is to extract the most appropriate polarisation of the issues. It is for this reason that the premature adoption of a point of view can be dangerous. With the use of more erasure than pencil lead, the thoughts should be redrafted into their 'rough' order. At this point more descriptive sentences should emerge.

3 The next stage is to prepare a final draft. With good fortune it might prove to be the finished product, but more likely it will be the penultimate draft. This is the stage at which one needs to be as self-critical as possible, to watch for assumptions that are not adequately supported, to tone down any bias that has crept in, to visualise the questions of critics, in short, to achieve balance.

4 Most drafts need shortening before they are written in their final form. Eliminate superfluous words and be your own editor.

5 Finally, *never* allow a report to leave the office without checking and always read it before signing. Be particularly wary of situations where a client wants a report in a hurry. On one occasion damages exceeding £700,000 were awarded against a firm for a negligent report.

6 A picrture, diagram or chart can be worth a thousand words while simultaneously enhancing the report's readability. Recent advances in document-copying equipment have brought these aids within the reach of every office, and they should be used to the full.

A report is normally sent with a letter, which is the proper place to thank the client for the instructions given and to mention matters relating to fees. A report should not be qualified in the accompanying letter in case it is passed on to a third party who would then remain unaware of the reservation.

Forms Filling out forms, often an irritating ritual, is a useful method of standardising communications, which simultaneously acts as a valuable checklist. However, forms can irritate people unless well laid out, and most need periodic re-design as circumstances change. Occasional checking of completed forms will often reveal that they are not being properly completed.

Mass media

Notice boards Where large numbers of people are involved, the notice board is an extremely economic method of speedy communication. It is, however, susceptible to abuse when used for the display of perfunctory instructions by tactless people. Alert management should watch the tone of announcements and instructions to ensure that they are a true reflection of their intended tone.

House journals The benefits of house journals have been the subject of debate over the years. Many an accountant, engaged on a cost reduction exercise, has allowed a malevolent gaze to fall on the office of the house journal's editor. Where an organisation is geographically dispersed (for example, in banking), the house journal represents one of the few methods available for keeping everyone informed about the social and business life of colleagues. A well conducted house journal can build a sense of unity of purpose, and at the same time give the families of staff and clients of the firm an insight into the company's affairs. In the final analysis it is the quality of the journal and the sincerity with which it is produced that will determine its success.

Films, television, slides and tape recordings Films and closed-circuit television generally require professional skills to produce results of an acceptable standard. They are costly. Nevertheless, they remain one of the best means of communication, and when opportunities exist for repetitive screening, they can be economic. Modern closed-circuit video-tape apparatus has greatly simplified production and increased the number of organisations that can benefit from its use. The potential of this equipment has not yet been fully appreciated, but doubtless the future will see an increase in its application for selling, technical education and 'in-house' training. The wide availability of cassette tape recorders has brought new opportunities for professional training. For many who are obliged to spend long periods driving, it has opened up opportunities for study and self-tuition. New legislation, technical papers, open university and radio talks can be recorded and played for easy learning during otherwise wasted time. Instructions for new staff and training talks can be recorded and circulated with consequent reductions in training costs and a greater feeling of personal involvement. The burden of reading can be reduced.

Summary

The letter, the memorandum, the everyday discussion are the vital signals that travel along the nervous system of commerce and professional life. If they are carelessly transmitted, wrongly routed, misunderstood or ineptly handled, the integrity and efficiency of the whole is put at risk. As an organisation grows in size or a subject increases in complexity, opportunities for error increase. Effective communication is a powerful tool for professional people. But the volume of communication that is handled is so great that it is too easily taken for granted, with potentially calamitous results in such areas as marketing, labour relations and contracts. In the medical world, life itself may be put at risk. Effective communication enables one to delegate and decentralise, both essential in the creation of large undertakings. Effective speaking, writing and listening are the links between the professional's brain and his clients'. If they are defective, his performance must be reduced.

Checklist – Chapter 7

COMMUNICATIONS

1 Does the firm place an emphasis on the subject of communication commensurate with the activity in which it is engaged?
2 What contact is maintained with the general public through its professional body in order to detect the change in demand and monitor the suitability of services offered?
3 What standard of communication is maintained with providers of the firm's capital?
4 Are communications between the profession and government adequate?
5 Are communications with employees and prospective entrants to the profession sound?
6 What is the 'public image' of the profession in the eyes of related professions, between the professional practitioners and their professional body, and among member firms?
7 What standard of communication takes place between the firm and its clients, between management and staff and among the partners themselves?
8 What volume and type of communications does the firm engage in?
9 What is the content of this communication?
10 Does the system, as operated, impose any risk to the client or to the firm?
11 Do the staff, managers, executives and partners all realise the importance of communication?
12 Is correspondence monitored by managers or partners?
13 Does the firm have sufficient telephone communications both internally and externally?

14 Are telephone operators handling the firm's business with efficiency?
15 Are internal and external meetings conducted in a businesslike way?
16 Does the firm's notepaper align with its general standards?
17 Does the firm issue a magazine or house journal, and if so, is it of satisfactory quality?
18 Does the firm utilise the services of a public relations consultant, and if not, would there be any advantages in so doing?
19 Are managers and executives trained in the conduct of meetings with clients; are agendas and minutes properly circulated?
20 Are reports to clients and internal reports to the partners of a good standard, or do they indicate an off-hand attitude to controls?
21 Do any of the members of the firm engage in outside activities, e.g. lecturing?
22 Are correspondence files maintained to a high standard?
23 Are the firm's 'archives' organised in such a way that documents and correspondence can be readily retrieved?
24 Is the system for controlling the destruction of files and documents satisfactory?

'Experience is the name everyone gives to their mistakes.'

Oscar Wilde

CHAPTER 8

The professional as manager and executive

A natural progression for men who prove to have ability is firstly into management within their specialised subject, and thereafter to general management within a practice. There are exceptions. In the sciences, in the law and indeed in the performing arts some people prefer to stay in their originally chosen field, becoming progressively more specialised throughout their career. Others find the call of teaching or the practice of consultancy stronger than the attractions of management. It may enable them to delve more deeply into their work and provide an opportunity for the development of new techniques. Much will depend on the individual's preference. But for those in private practice a common ambition is to join the partnership of an existing firm or to found their own business.

This decision is of importance in the progress of a career and one that should be approached by both the employer and the professional with thought. Some firms repeatedly promote the best man without properly training him for his enlarged responsibilities until they reach the point at which he fails. Similarly it is a fault in many ambitious young men to seek advancement primarily on the strength of their professional skill without, at the same time, developing their management capabilities. Training before promotion is greatly undervalued by many. In those of less than average management capability, promotion is sometimes sought by changing from employer to employer rather than by progressing within the firm. Equally some employers, having failed to develop existing staff for promotion, are obliged to look elsewhere when senior vacancies occur, thereby demoralising existing staff and often experiencing disappointment in their choice. The assumption that success in a particular discipline automatically confers an ability to plan and coordinate the activities of others, and to be successful in the various techniques of management, is ill-founded.

Training for management

Management is one of the most challenging and rewarding business activities. But it makes considerable demands on a person's physical and mental strength, and preparation is necessary, particularly where the span of responsibilities is large, the speed of events under his control is high or the matters which he manages are controversial. The price for inadequate training may be paid by the employer in the form of reduced performance and even by losses, but there is a price too that is paid personally by the inadequate manager in the form of worry, excessive strain, unnecessarily long working hours and sometimes failure. In many general management situations a specialist's skill actually recedes in importance, and the individual may find that he is progressively losing touch with his original subject as daily management responsibilities increase and his professional judgement of detail is less frequently used. It is not unknown for this tendency to go too far and for senior managers who have become out of touch with the developments in their original discipline to acquire a subconscious opposition to new ideas put forward by enthusiastic and 'inexperienced' youngsters.

The training programme should therefore be directed towards acquisition of management capability and, as circumstances require, a continuation of training in the original disciplines. What then are the qualities that a man needs the first day after this promotion when he takes on a management role? There are a number. Of paramount importance is the fact that he will be obliged to accept and handle a greatly changed set of relationships with other people. In the past he may have been preoccupied only with his personal performance, with improving his status in the eyes of his immediate superiors and with gaining the position that he has now acquired. Now, as a manager, he will be judged not only on his personal contribution but on the achievements of those he controls. In the past his work may have been planned for him; now he must plan his own work, delegate and take responsibility for those for whom he is accountable. In the past he was probably supervised and advised on how to go about his work; now the task is his.

The day of receiving corrective instructions is past, and he must accustom himself to observing and correcting others. His relationship with his subordinates, who until recently may have been his colleagues, will change. His relationship to the organisation as a whole will alter. His seniors of yesterday may now be his equals. Past alliances will weaken and may be embarrassing and new alliances will be made. Hopefully he will realise that these new relationships will require cultivation for they may have to stand the test of years. Finally, there will be changes within himself as his sights are raised to the next objective in his career, his horizons expand, his responsibilities increase and his concern for his subordinates brings him into increasing contact with responsibility. It is a testing time and the changes are far more subtle than may be symbolised by a larger and shinier motor car or a longer lunch hour in more congenial surroundings.

The problems of the new manager

Because general managers have to cover a wider range of subjects, it is a mind-stretching process. Because they have to think increasingly in terms of plans for the future, it extends the use of the imagination. Because the consequences of error become progressively greater with seniority, it is a maturing process.

A failure to appreciate the extent of these changes sometimes leads the new manager, and those who are not so new, into two common errors:

1 The manager believes that all he has to do is to set a good example for others to follow.
2 He sees the solution of all problems in terms of his original specialisation.

This is frequent in industry and is characterised by the former salesman who, on assuming wider responsibilities, can be heard proclaiming that the destiny of the organisation is best served by enlarging and streamlining the sales force and such activities as construction of new showrooms of even greater magnificence. Similarly the former marketing man may see the path to greater profitability in a programme of beautifying the company's image and creating of a vast new range of products. The former engineer invariably knows ways of increasing profit with new machinery, and the former accountant may want to get rid of everything he cannot count or prove beyond doubt to be profitable.

On occasions this kind of reorientation can be exactly what the company needs and in the short term produce admirable results. But it is a dangerous way of achieving them and a difficult process to reverse or alter. In addition this type of bias tends to reduce inter-departmental cooperation, and investment plans can go awry and remain so long after the erring manager has left the scene. Many organisations are occupied with the rectification of at least one problem, and often more, caused by imbalance in previous management.

The development of management skill

Where the executive or new manager is fortunate, he will have already received training for his new work. His immediate superior, by process of delegation and example, will have prepared him. Attention will have been directed to the following:

1 The development of a wider, more open and objective approach to his work and the adoption of a broader view of his firm.
2 Cultivation of his ability to organise himself and to communicate.

3 Development of the talent of planning, organisation, review and control of the activities, people and assets for which he is responsible.
4 Improvement of the skill of decision-making.
5 A watchfulness to avoid errors of excessive pride, envy and personality problems, and an increased resistance to the manoeuvres and games people play in building defences and seeking personal advantages.

Development of the right attitude

No training programme can form attitudes — they are innate to the individual — but it can condition attitudes and should do so. It is important to ensure that newly promoted managers and executives have a healthy view of the firm as a whole. There is not much chance of rising above mediocrity if there is no real pride in the firm's past history or ambition for its future.

A person of initiative will have read about the history of his profession and know something of the development of the firm for whom he is working. He will perhaps have to discard his old departmental loyalties. One famous judge, on being asked to comment on the change that took place when he left the Bar for the Bench, spoke about the isolation of the position of the judge and the fact that he had to acquire the art of listening more, sitting still for long periods of time and speaking less. On the same theme some captains of aircraft have commented that the loneliest man on a large jet aircraft is often the man in command.

Self-organisation

It is noticeable that the most efficient managers are frequently those with the most time to spare. The first step towards success in management is success in self-management. It is probable during the period immediately following their promotion that they will not have enough time to do all the work they want to. This will bring them face to face with the problem of delegation. This subject was covered at some length when dealing with organisation. Delegation is an essential function of management. The executive who fails to acquire the art will quickly find that his time is dissipated with tasks that should be done by his subordinates.

The input of work to a manager varies widely, but customarily appears in the form of a stream of paperwork into an 'in' tray, a succession of phone calls and a series of personal contacts. The first step is to deal with the work input in a logical fashion and seek to control it before priorities become obscure. The following hints may be useful:

1 It is impossible to allocate priority either in dealing with incoming matters or in delegation if the overall priorities of the job are not understood. It is necessary for each manager to have a complete understanding of his own job specification if he is to order his affairs to advantage.

2 In deciding what proportion of incoming work to delegate, he must have an accurate idea of the time he has available for carrying out his own duties. This involves a study over a period of days, weeks or even months so that he can relieve himself by delegation of a sufficient amount of work to leave him with adequate time to deal with those things with which only he can deal.

3 A common mistake is to be drawn into too much detailed examination of a matter which is subsequently going to be delegated, at the expense of time that should be spent on the broader issues and planning the assignment. The handling of incoming work can be simplified by developing a personal checklist designed to ensure that all the information necessary for dealing with the matter has been provided or is available. It is unfortunate when a matter, having sat in the 'in' tray for a week, has to be referred back for further information which was lacking when the item first arrived.

Another advantage of a good sense of priorities arises from the fact that few matters can be dealt with in the order of their arrival. Where the sorting process is efficient, it greatly speeds the handling of the work input. Many people hesitate too long before delegating and then put undue pressure on the person ultimately doing the work because of the delay that has occured.

4 A cause of considerable fatigue arises not so much out of the execution of the work itself but in the excessive and rapid switching of the mind from subject to subject. Each time a new matter has to be considered, the memory has to recall the history, surrounding facts and necessary knowledge. It is for this reason that repeated interruptions are fatiguing and that a great reward accrues to the person who can organise his work by grouping the consideration of subjects through the organisation of his diary. A helpful exercise is to study the allocation of one's time. It is unlikely that one will be able to achieve an ideal balance, but it will form the basis of planning daily and weekly work and of dealing with those items which recur at intervals throughout the calendar. It also helps in understanding the process of delegation.

5 In studying activities the busy manager should be in search of work that can be eliminated, delegated or simplified without affecting performance. Items that occur regularly can sometimes be rationalised by use of a standard procedure or of a checklist and be rendered into a form which permits delegation previously thought impractical. Time spent standardising a procedure for dealing with recurrent items saves a great deal of effort. Much professional work requires concentration, and if excessive interruptions occur, unnecessary fatigue results and the quality of work is reduced, in some cases to a point of danger. The training of secretaries and assistants and the organisation of a diary to provide set periods when interruptions are restricted and the manager is able to concentrate on one job at a time are essential. While communications need to be efficient, they also need to be orderly.

6 The method of handling visitors depends largely on the nature of the work. Wherever possible, subordinates should be encouraged to fix specific times for meetings and to give prior notice of the subjects they wish to discuss. This gives the

manager the opportunity to specify any information that he will require at the meeting and also serves to remind the subordinate to prepare his material properly. The manager has to achieve a balance, according to his function and seniority, between inaccessibility and total accessibility. Efficiency is impeded by those of hermit-like disposition, but equally there is a danger of a team falling into the bad habit of popping their heads round each other's doors to deal with trivialities.

7 Where the manager finds he is spending excessive time giving instructions to his subordinates on the way in which work is to be carried out, it may indicate inadequacy in their training. It sometimes requires considerable self-discipline, particularly when one is working under pressure, to set time aside for the training of staff in order to increase delegation. But when one calculates the cost of management time, it is a task that should not be deferred.

Routine

Each individual varies and rules are difficult to make. Some people find their most creative hours are late in the day, others find them early in the morning. An executive should know his activity pattern and adjust his daily routine accordingly. Wherever possible some physical activity should break up desk work. Long hours sitting at a desk without any physical movement are, to many people, dulling. Managers are often obliged to travel great distances, and journeys and rest periods should be planned. No enlightened employer can be genuinely thankful to an executive whose enthusiasm causes him to drive for excessive periods. Proper breaks should be achieved in any journey, and the long, late-night drive home after a heavy day and a social hour should be avoided. No sensible employer should habitually expect a man to be a hundred miles from his base one day and back at his desk the following morning.

The diary should, as far as possible, be a carefully planned programme of work and not a book in which one is always searching for blank spaces in which to squeeze appointments. The executive should make his own appointments and not allow his secretary to become his work planner unless it is on an agreed basis.

Decision-making

Indecision is one of the greatest causes of insomnia. It is an equally frequent cause of procrastination, particularly where the action to be taken involves difficulties in human relations or the consequences are likely to be unpleasant. The manager cannot hope to achieve a comfortable position until he has mastered the procedure of decision-making. For some it presents little difficulties; for others it requires training and self-discipline. The first step is to define the problem accurately. Quick decisions made on rapid assessments are, as often as not, bad decisions made about the wrong problem. In any but the simplest matters it is likely that the definition of the problem will be improved if it is written down. It may seem a waste of time, but it is surprising how problems change their shape when committed to writing. The next step is to decide on the information that is necessary in order to start an evaluation. Where this information is to be drawn from others, it is important to ensure that they are given an accurately stated question and all the information necessary for them to make an effective contribution. The objective thinker will be particularly careful not to load or slant the questions in order to produce an answer pleasing to himself.

Having gathered all the necessary information, it will be possible to identify the different courses open, and to programme and cost the events arising from each. In this process such formal techniques as 'decision trees' can be of great assistance. The initial phase of the decision-making process is often similar to the brain storming or research stage of report writing. The more open the mind, the better. The greater the range of alternatives that can be devised, the more thorough the investigation will be. One course of action that should always be included is to do nothing. There is a delightful range of reasons for inactivity, and examples abound in the statements reported in the daily press. For example, 'the matter is premature'; 'the proposals are impractical'; 'the problem is exaggerated'; 'various solutions are currently being considered'; 'a decision and statement will be made in due course'.

Judgement can only be made after a thorough investigation of the alternatives and consequences. Consequences can normally be expressed in terms of physical results, impact on organisation, impact on clients or patients, effects on staff, results in terms of financial advantage or loss, cost effectiveness, convenience and speed. It is often tempting to leap from the problem to the solution without considering the means. The resources at a manager's command are normally limited, and effort can usually be diverted along different lines. The solution of nearly every problem involves the diversion of resources in terms of manpower, money and assets from an activity upon which they would otherwise be engaged. In taking a comprehensive view of situations in the decision-making process, it is necessary to think in terms of the effect of the decision on those above and below and at the same level, and of the consumption of available resources. When considering communications and report writing, reference was made to reading High Court judgements. Apart from their interest and high standard and the elegance of language which they frequently display, they are an excellent example of the decision-making process. Non-legal students in the professions can benefit greatly by visiting the courts and watching the court procedure and listening to the judgements during their early career. When possible it is better to read the full law report rather than the edited versions found in magazines. Finally the decision, when made, should be delivered with as little reservation as possible and with as much conviction as the individual can summon up. Bad decision-makers sometimes behave like bad chess players, tentatively touching and moving pieces, each time looking up to see the reaction of the other player. In business, as in chess, once the move is decided upon, it should be made with a sure hand.

Planning and review

The subject of planning, organisation and review forms

separate chapters. The individual manager's personal work is equally subject to this process. Careful planning probably increases personal effectiveness more than any other activity, and the periodic review of one's personal performance is the key to its improvement. An artist can be coached to a high level of competence by others, but those that go on to develop their talent into a highly individual or unique form usually base each forward step upon self-criticism of their progress to that point. The development of management talent can be accelerated by training, but the final emergence of the power of leadership depends largely on that cycle of review, experiment and improvement that can only be conducted within the minds of those with the intellect and personality to become true leaders.

In the process of self-review the manager should watch for common failings — common not to managers in particular, but to all human beings. For example:

1 Excessive optimism. Without a measure of optimism many of us would probably give up. There are those who habitually describe a glass as half-full and those who would say it was half-empty. Nothing is more sapping to morale than the gloomy team member. But excessive optimism is a failing that can lead the small businessman into difficulty in over-estimating his performance, the capability of his team, the time that a project may take or the profits to be made from a particular venture.

2 The balance between literacy and numeracy has been the subject of comment in recent years by many observers of managers' performance. The original, eloquent and forceful are sometimes able to persuade both themselves and others to follow courses of action which on the most elementary mathematical or financial analysis would prove to be doomed. Most business decisions require evaluation in both words and figures. The balance varies according to the task, but most good ideas need support by carefully worked figures, just as most carefully worked figures need explanation with words.

3 Favouritism is quickly sensed by subordinates and inhibits both teamwork and loyalty — to the cost of the manager. Total

impartiality is impossible, and probably undesirable, but it is a responsibility of a manager to be scrupulously fair in his dealings with his subordinates.

4 A rather nebulous concept, but one which has often occurred to the writer, is that of 'keeping in step'. Some managers are frequently heard to complain that those behind them are too thrusting, that those in front of them are too slow, that those above lack understanding and those beneath them are not worth trusting. All joint endeavour is based on the individual members keeping roughly in step, and as the professional person develops his management capability, he may do well to ask himself if he is achieving this.

5 The attainment of good relationships with clients is of obvious importance. In reviewing personal progress it is necessary to check on the quality of relationships achieved and the level of confidence that clients display. It has often been said that it is a fault in a professional person to identify himself with his client's problems because it destroys objectivity. But, equally, detachment can lead the client to the erroneous conclusion that the adviser 'doesn't really care'. It is a complaint often heard about some professional people, and when it is justified it must indicate a weakness in the development of good client relations.

Summary

There are no magic rules to guide a manager. There are guidelines and well known pitfalls. What is certain is that training is necessary if a person is to develop to his full potential. Every professional practice, every professional practitioner and every organisation depend to a great extent on the quality of their managers. The value of service given to the general public and the reputation of the profession as a whole is conditioned by the standard of management skill within that profession. In pursuing improvement, every technique merits examination, for skill in the application of knowledge is often as important and sometimes more important than the knowledge itself.

Checklist – Chapter 8

THE PROFESSIONAL AS MANAGER AND EXECUTIVE

1 What demands are made of the professional as a manager and executive?
2 Will his career pattern afford opportunities which are primarily of a management nature?
3 For what numbers of people and resources will he become responsible as his career progresses?
4 Is adequate training given before promotion?
5 Are vacancies which carry management responsibility normally filled from within the organisation or by recruitment?
6 Do executives or managers within the organisation habitually work overtime?
7 Do management responsibilities render it difficult to keep up-to-date with developments in the original discipline?
8 Do newly appointed managers have any difficulty in adjusting to the new relationships with their staff, peers and partners?
9 Have the managers and executives achieved satisfactory confidence in delegation?
10 Do managers display good standards of self-management?
11 Is the flow of incoming work to the firm well organised?
12 Do the managers have a good sense of priority in handling the work input?
13 Are visitors received and handled well?
14 Have managers received any training in the decision-making process, and do delays occur as a result of deferred decisions?

15 Are managers planning their departmental activities well in advance?

16 Are managers participating in the overall development of the firm's plans?

17 How frequently do managers fail to achieve forecast performance?

18 Do junior staff have a good morale?

'Money speaks sense in a language all nations understand'.

Anon

CHAPTER 9

Financial management

No matter how small a business is, it must think in terms of figures and have adequate financial controls or it will not survive. This will be self-evident to those professions concerned with commerce, but there are many which are quite remote from finance and some to whom its workings remain a mystery. All professional firms must attain good financial management if they are to grow in value. In addition there are some that give advice that may have important financial implications for their clients who may be considerably larger in size, so that for many professional people an appreciation of larger-scale industrial financial management is necessary in addition to the requirements for their own smaller-scale affairs. Apart from the statutory obligations to keep books of account, some professions with fiduciary responsibilities are also obliged to conform to rules laid down by their governing bodies, the breach of which can bring serious consequences.

The sophistication of financial management within a firm will depend upon its size, the importance attached to it by the partners, the nature of the work undertaken and the demands of the work for financial control. It varies greatly and can be best illustrated by looking at varying degrees of elaboration commonly encountered. The sole practitioner or small firm may take the traditional view that it amounts to little more than keeping an eye on the bank balance, raising invoices and paying bills, keeping elementary books and dealing with returns for value added tax — the annual accounts being dealt with by their accountant. The practice may be relatively safe in financial terms and the demands of the proprietors sufficiently modest to ensure liquidity and an annual surplus. Frequently finance is dealt with by the senior partner assisted by a part-time bookeeper. There may seem to be little need for a budget, and proposed capital expenditure will be dealt with on an *ad hoc* basis. Moving on to a slightly larger firm, one may find a senior partner in charge assisted by a full-time accountant, who may also deal with other administrative matters. Financial reports, or at least summaries of selected key figures, will be prepared at intervals for the partners and there may be an elementary budget. Up to this point the firm is still of such size that it can be managed by personal supervision and controlled by inspection, and the financial affairs of the business will be easy to comprehend.

However, there is a point where it is difficult to manage by inspection and controls must be expanded. Policies and plans will become necessary for the management of capital, handling taxation, the control of expenditure, the evaluation of progress in the different departments and activities, the levels of fees to be charged and the control of the assets. At this stage the financial function is no longer a matter of accounting for past events but extends to planning for future activities. Failure to develop the financial management capability in step with, if not ahead of, the firm's needs can leave it dangerously exposed to the risks of overtrading, payment of unnecessarily high rates of interest on borrowed money, surprise tax demands and loss of control. Furthermore, as the partners and departments grow in number, so too will the need to place the management of finance in the hands of one person who can maintain a balanced, impartial and overall view of progress and the future. In large-scale commercial activities one often finds this important work being carried out by a director of finance or controller to whom the chief accountant reports and who in turn advises the board of directors in this area. Such an organisation focuses the attention of all concerned on the financial implications of all proposals and decisions, and increases the emphasis on the future while simultaneously ensuring proper control of current activity.

Responsibilities of the financial manager

In a similar way, the partner responsible for finance has a very important contribution to make, and his responsibilities will include, in addition to liason with the firm's auditors in producing the annual accounts, the following management functions:

1 Management accounting

For the partners or directors to control the business they must know, at appropriate intervals, the overall position of the firm and its component parts and the significant trends that may prompt action. This raises a number of questions:

a What information should be gathered which will most vividly and economically communicate the past progress.

b How should it be presented in order that busy colleagues can make their best contribution?

c How frequently should the information be distributed in order to avoid debasing it by excessive reporting, while still ensuring that it is circulated in time for remedial action when necessary?

d How should the work be organised and, where appropriate, delegated? Staff may be adequate for the entire process to be carried out internally, or the firm's auditors may periodically supplement the work of the bookkeeper.

The gathering, interpretation and communication of this information involves the design of one of the most important control systems and an opportunity for the use of imagination. As was seen in considering *Control and Review* the information must highlight *performance*. In this respect ratios* can be far more valuable than figures taken in isolation and trends in ratios far more illuminating than columns of isolated figures.

*For more, see G.A. Westwick, *How to Use Management Ratios*, Gower Press.

But even ratios in isolation need a bench mark for comparison and these may be:

1 The firm's past performance.
2 Comparison with budgets and forecasts.
3 Comparison with other firms where figures are published or can be obtained by confidential exchange.
4 Through the firm's accountants who may have developed opinions in handling similar clients.

Ratios of value include:

1 To indicate the trend in volume of business:

$$\frac{\text{Gross fees earned this period}}{\text{Gross fees earned in previous year in same period}}$$

2 To indicate the position of the 'order' book and warn of any reduction in future work loads or necessary increases in establishment:

$$\frac{\text{Value of work outstanding}}{\text{Average value of work done per month}}$$

3 To expose trends in individual departmental performance and changes in the nature of the work undertaken, the ratio given in (1) above should be determined for each department or function.

4 To enable the partners to compare the return on their investment with alternatives and to expose the efficiency of the enterprise, determine the following ratio:

$$\frac{\text{Net profit after tax and payment of notional partners' salaries}}{\text{Capital of the firm}}$$

5 The cost of external capital may prompt a search for cheaper sources. The lower the following ratio, the cheaper the cost of capital:

$$\frac{\text{Interest paid on borrowed money}}{\text{Borrowed capital}}$$

6 To indicate the ability of the firm to meet its obligations:

$$\frac{\text{Cash + Debtors + Securities}}{\text{Borrowed capital}}$$

7 To highlight the cost of debtors:

$$\frac{\text{Debtors}}{\text{Average daily charges}}$$

This ratio should be studied in conjunction with (5) above.

8 To reveal the vital factor of profit:

$$\frac{\text{Net profit}}{\text{Gross fees earned}}$$

9 To reveal any improvements in the handling of tax affairs and keep management aware of the impact of taxation:

$$\frac{\text{Taxation}}{\text{Net profit before tax}}$$

10 To indicate the liquidity of the firm and forewarn of illiquidity caused by overtrading:

$$\frac{\text{Current assets}}{\text{Current liabilities}}$$

11 The following ratio is vital in the highly labour-intensive professions and changes may trigger adjustments to fees charged:

$$\frac{\text{Personnel costs}}{\text{Average number of employees}}$$

In addition, ratios may be devised to indicate such features as:

12 The profit per partner.
13 The gross fees per partner.
14 The cost of staff as a proportion of total fees earned.

15 The cost of staff in relation to profits.
16 Overheads as a percentage of total fees.
17 Cost of accommodation as a percentage of fees.
18 Cost of transport as a percentage of fees.
19 Cost of equipment as a percentage of fees.
20 Partner's maximum, minimum and average drawings.
21 Staff turnover.
22 Cost of professional indemnity as a percentage of labour costs.
23 Ratio of the cost of non-productive or support staff to fee-earning staff.

A study of each business will be necessary to reveal which factors are significant and reveal the trends that need to be observed. To economise, the partner responsible may devise a system where only variances from a predetermined magnitude are reported. Graphs may be more vivid than columns of figures and with modern copiers are easily updated and circulated.

2 Appointment of the firm's auditors

The partner responsible will wish to ensure that the firm is getting the best advice and that the accountants are efficient. In this capacity he becomes a purchaser of professional services and will settle their brief, fees and any additional services that may be needed on taxation or finance.

3 Cash control

Treasurership, as it is sometimes called, involves the planning and control of cash to ensure that the firm is always able to meet its commitments. This cannot be done without forecasting furture expenditure and fees that will be earned, a matter that needs continual attention, particularly in younger and less substantially capitalised firms.

The firm's selection of bankers and the relationship with them come within the financial partner's responsibilities, and changes may be necessary if the service received falls short of its needs or changing bank staff reduce the standard of the relationship, which should always be maintained at a high level by good communication.

4 Credit control

Some professionals find that their reticence to chase debtors for 'professional' reasons is exploited to the full. Firm and tactful handling will be necessary to avoid an excessive problem with debtors. The larger firm may have to create a policy for the guidance of departmental managers and supervise its implementation.

5 Purchasing

The best terms must always be negotiated for the acquisition of all premises, equipment and supplies, and this may involve an assessment of the relative advantages of leasing, hire-purchase, rental and outright purchase. This will need a knowledge of the firm's capital structure and present and future cash position. Where property is concerned, the benefits of purchase as opposed to leasing may raise the matter of the partners' investment and lead to a forecast of capital gains that might be available to offset inflation or through the release of development potential.

6 Costing

Where charges to clients are determined by reference to scale fees, which in recent years has become illegal in some professions, the fees present no difficulty. In fact such professions have sometimes enjoyed a growth in fee income related not to their own increased costs but to those of a related industry or market. For example estate agents' fees were swollen by the property boom, and architects' incomes grew as a percentage of rising building costs. However, where fees are charged on the basis of time taken or *quantum meruit*, then records will be needed so that each assignment can be accurately costed. Busy professional people are sometimes loathe to keep mileage and expense records and time sheets, and tempers may fray in maintaining a regular system. In the case of *quantum meruit* charges (how much he has deserved), the value of services rendered colours the fee, and judgement will be needed to place a premium or allow a discount on a pure time charge.

The overall costs of running the firm and each department or fee-earning individual must be known if charges are to be fair and performance measured accurately. The closest analysis of costs is particularly important in times of inflation as under-charged fees represent a loss that cannot be recovered. An assessment of the profitability of each activity is also necessary in the decision-making processes that take place in devising marketing policy, manning levels, salary scales and bonuses. So far in this chapter accounting has been the chief concern, that is to say, achieving a true, fair, consistent and conservative view of the firm's financial progress and position. In navigation it is important to know one's point of origin and present position, but there remains the problem of the rest of the voyage before one arrives safely at the destination. For this reason the navigator spends much of his time considering the alternative routes for the remainder of the journey and identifying those hazards of current, tide and coastline that are ahead and need to be taken into account by the captain.

This analogy underscores an important distinction between simple accounting and financial management in the wider sense of the word. It is also a useful reminder that the rougher the weather, the more frail the boat or the more intricate the navigation, so proportionately greater is the need for foresight and accuracy. This brings up the subject of financial planning.

Financial planning

The financial manager will have participated in, and hopefully contributed to, the creation of the firm's long-term plans and will have given financial expression to its objectives. These will be expressed in terms of a profit plan for the whole firm and each department or function upon which it relies. He will personally have given deep thought to whether these ambitions are realistic, and will have calculated the growth rates and profits necessary to provide the physical and working capital involved. In short he will have satisfied himself that his colleagues are treading a carefully planned path. Because this work has been done, the partnership will have a profit consciousness.

Longer-term plans for the purchase of freeholds or equipment or for expansion will not in themselves be adequate, for in the short term much more detail will be necessary if month-by-month control is to be maintained. For this purpose budgets will be needed. These are usually drawn up for a period of a year. If a standard form can be devised and printed, it will prove helpful and reduce the risk of omissions. If costs can be grouped into logical headings that match the firm's structure, reference is easier. By extension the figures can be apportioned to departments where appropriate. Such a schedule is set out below:

Fixed establishment costs

Rent, etc.

1.1 Rent.
1.2 Rent increases.
1.3 Landlord's service charges.
1.4 Landlord's insurance charges.
1.5 Landlord's legal or licence charges.
1.6 Mortgage interest.
1.7 Mortgage repayments.

Rates

1.8 General rates.
1.9 Water rates.
1.10 Provision for increases during the year.

Services and utilities

1.11 Electricity.
1.12 Gas.

1.13 Contract waste removal.
1.14 Security services.
1.15 Janitorial services.

Maintenance
1.22 Grounds, paths, roads and fences.
1.23 Exterior painting.
1.24 Interior decoration.
1.25 Exterior repairs.
1.26 Interior repairs.
1.27 Fire detection and sprinkler equipment.
1.28 Life maintenance.
1.29 Reserve for dilapidations at the termination of leases.

Cleaning
1.30 Windows and signs.
1.31 Interiors.
1.32 Towel and linen hire or laundry.

Insurance

2.1 Premises.
2.2 Contents and equipment.
2.3 All risks.
2.4 Employers' liability.
2.5 Professional indemnity.
2.6 Travel risks.
2.7 Third party.
2.8 Health — accidents.
2.9 Private cars.
2.10 Fidelity bonding.

Office expenses

3.1 Printed stationery.
3.2 Special printing — forms, etc.,
3.3 Photocopying, plan printing and duplicating.
3.4 General stationery supplies.

3.5 Office equipment hire and maintenance.
3.6 Magazines and newspapers.
3.7 Depreciation on furniture.
3.8 Depreciation on equipment.
3.9 Petty cash and refreshments.

Communications

4.1 Telephones.
4.2 Telex and cables.
4.3 Postage.

External services

5.1 Accountants and auditors and annual returns.
5.2 Solicitors.
5.3 Professional bodies.
5.4 Annual licences.

Salaries

(Gross costs including increases, bonuses, commissions and pension costs)
6.1 Partners.
6.2 Fee-earning and qualified staff.
6.3 Technical assistants.
6.4 Clerical staff.
6.5 Other employees.
6.6 Terminations.
6.7 Recruitment advertising.
6.8 Employment bureaux.
6.9 Training — 'in house'.
6.10 Training — external.

Note: This category of cost may be additionally analysed by function.

Transport

7.1 Depreciation of cars.
7.2 Maintenance, cleaning and tyres.
7.3 Fuels and lubricants.
7.4 Road fund licences.
7.5 Motoring associations.
7.6 Parking and fines.
7.7 Contingency for accidents.
7.8 Car hire.

Public transport and accommodation

8.1 Trains, buses, taxis.
8.2 Planes and sea travel.
8.3 Accommodation.
8.4 Out-of-pocket expenses.
8.5 Entertaining.

Research and development and equipment

9.1 Maintenance of reference library.
9.2 Maintenance of technical equipment.
9.3 Depreciation of technical equipment.
9.4 Laboratory or technical materials.
9.5 Materials consumed.

Marketing

10.1 Market research — published information.
10.2 Market research — purchased information.
10.3 Surveys.
10.4 Design and research into new services or products.
10.5 Test marketing costs.

Selling

11.1 Advertising, newspapers, magazines, special journals.
11.2 Promotions and gifts.
11.3 Direct mail.
11.4 Signs and hoardings.
11.5 Editorial publicity.
11.6 Exhibitions.

Where a budget on the foregoing lines is prepared, standardisation of the category reference numbers can simplify the allocation of costs in the analysis of purchases. It can also be used as the basis of standing instructions for the bookkeeping staff. Similar budgets will be necessary to deal with proposed capital purchases and disposals before the total expenditure side of the business can be seen in its entirety.

It is seldom that all partners are equally aware or concerned by financial matters; it would be a dull world if they were. An important by-product of detailed budgeting is to draw the partners together on this subject. Additionally it enables the partners to inform department managers accurately about the costs of operations in their control, and it places the subject of salary administration in perspective. Budgets are also a necessary basis for comparison in studying the management ratios previously referred to, as target ratios can be established in advance. Finally they help to avoid the danger of overspending or overdrawing when there are cash surpluses that should be kept in reserve for future liabilities or taxation, for which separate budgets should be maintained. However, it is important to take into account the fact that the preparation of detailed budgets is a useless exercise if subsequent performance is not continually measured against the budget.

Summary

The financial manager who is in real command of the finances of a firm is in a position to make a contribution to nearly every important management decision. In assessing the merits of ideas put forward, he will be working on the sure footing provided by knowledge of the firm's current and expected profits, considering its present break-even level for gross fees brought in and the impact of a failed project on reserves.

However, finance is a function that should contribute to management and not dominate or control it. Many management decisions involve judgement, the acceptance of calculated risk, and the valuation of intangible benefits. Financial aspects must be considered and duly weighed in the decision-making process and on occasions will determine the best course. However, management remains the responsibility of the partners or directors *as a whole* and should never be allowed to become the sole province of the counting house.

Checklist – Chapter 9

FINANCIAL MANAGEMENT

1 What level of sophistication does the size of the firm and nature of the work indicate *(a)* at present and *(b)* over the next few years.
2 Who is the financial manager and is the extent of the responsibility clearly defined?
3 Can finances be controlled by accounting and inspection or are additional controls necessary?
4 Are there any special accounting rules laid down by the professional body?
5 Is adequate information circulated to the partners at appropriate intervals and in time for remedial action when necessary?
6 Does circulated information portray a vivid picture of the firm's performance, as a whole and for each function or department?
7 How are fees calculated?
8 Do fees in all activities bear a proper relation to the costs of work undertaken?
9 Does the professional body take adequate interest in the financial management techniques and profitability of its members?
10 Does the firm prepare an adequate budget?
11 What external sources of information are available for comparison in assessing the firm's performance, e.g. published reports, professional institute guidelines, privately arranged exchanges of information?
12 Is the manager of each department kept aware of its progress?
13 What are the best ratios for revealing the firm's performance and are they used?

14 What is the brief given to the firm's accountants, and do they contribute to the extent that they could or should?
15 Is cash control satisfactory and secure?
16 Does the firm control its debtors satisfactorily?
17 Where the premises are owned or held under an advantageous lease by a minority of senior partners, do they subsidise other partners or charge a proper rent?
18 Are purchases handled formally and all available discounts obtained by negotiation?
19 How far in advance does the firm plan its finances?
20 Is the role of the financial manager properly appreciated, and does his calibre match the demands?
21 What is the quality of the firm's relationship with its bankers?

'It is the customer who determines what a business is. It is the customer alone whose willingness to pay for a good or service converts economic sources into wealth. . . .'

Peter Drucker

CHAPTER 10

Marketing and selling professional services

Too many professionals do not consider the marketing of their services an essential part of their practice, either because they consider it undignified or because they think it might result in a breach of the restrictions placed on them by their professional institute. However, market awareness — an awareness of customer needs and requirements, a search for customer identity, characteristics and location — is as vital to the professional practice as it is to industry and commerce.

Market research

This systematic activity collects and interprets fact and opinion about the products and services of a business. It is concerned with advertising, public relations, distribution and selling in the past, present and future. There can be little hope of achieving sound short-range decisions or, perhaps even more importantly, long-term investment decisions unless trends are understood. Research is not only confined to existing services; it examines clients' needs and their preferences. In a wider field it engages in overall market assessments, and seeks answers to such questions as the total number of potential clients, changes in their class and location, the size of the market, activities of competitors and the best means of getting the service to the client, i.e. distribution and availability.

It has been put somewhat bluntly that if a person wants to get his hands into the public's purse, he must first understand the public's mind. In industry the scale of business investment is now so great that management cannot risk the launch of a new project on hunch. The volume and organisation of production, recruitment of personnel, the long-range purchase of materials and other resources, the acquisition of premises and the scale of advertising will be dictated by sales forecasts. These in turn are based on research into the total market potential, the strength of competition, and assessment of the appeal of one's own output and the portion of the market that it might gain. This involves the examination of all the published statistics and may need statisticians to interpret accurately the data and forecast trends. Field work may also be needed to gather information on clients' tastes and intentions by interview and questionnaire. The process will vary in each case, and trained personnel may be necessary to ensure sound results. The purpose of the research should be thought out carefully. Typically this may be:

1 To assess the level of satisfaction being given by existing services and the range, cost and quality of competitors' services.
2 To seek ways of expanding the range of existing services.
3 To find new or emerging client needs, i.e. to identify new opportunities.
4 To detect areas of client misunderstanding or discontent.
5 To assess reaction to a proposed change in existing services or a new service or to estimate the volume of potential business.

The type of questions that will be preoccupying the researcher may be:

1 How large is the existing and potential market?
2 What factors govern demand for the service? What triggers demand?
3 What are the age, sex, class and other characteristics of existing and potential clients?
4 Where are these clients located?

5 Are those who do not use the service aware of the benefits they forego?
6 Why do people not use an available service that could be of value to them?
7 In the case of commercial clients, from what areas are they drawn?
8 What are the size and type of commercial clients?
9 What type of work do commercial clients generate?
10 Are any new services required by commercial clients to meet the demands on them created by:
   a New legislation.
   b Expansion and contraction or changing patterns of trade.
   c Regional growth and decline, the availability of grants or incentives and problems of regeneration and relocation.
   d Advances in technology, i.e. computer bureaux, etc.
11 Are there any innovations available through the combination of hitherto uncombined services to form new 'package' services, i.e. project management.
12 What pricing patterns exist in the market?

On a large scale such research may be undertaken by the appropriate professional body for the benefit of its members. But there is no reason why the individual firm should not tackle some of the basic and important questions in its attempts to respond to its environment in the most profitable way. What is important is that sound information about clients should be intelligently gathered and absorbed into the marketing process, which can then be used safely in evolving the firm's overall objectives. A good part of market research reveals a profession to itself as others see it; no matter how small or tarnished the mirror, it will usually evoke some measure of surprise. One thing is certain, and that is that a profession that does not maintain a programme of systematic research is probably making insincere or inaccurate claims about its importance and value to society.

Service strategy

This aspect of marketing is concerned with the selection and review of the services offered. It is the counterpart of the product strategy of a manufacturing company. Its aim is to select or to develop and maintain that range of services that will maximise the profitability and future growth of a firm. It involves the innovation or development of new services and the cessation of those with no further useful life or profitability.

This is an area in which one can encounter a marked difference between the professions and conventional commerce in the maintenance of unprofitable activities. It is frequently the case that a business offering a range of products achieves most of its sales and profit (perhaps over three-quarters) from a third or less of its range It is not uncommon to find that a measurable proportion of its products contributes little to profits and may even incur losses. Their continuance is due to a number of reasons:

1 The company does not realise the loss it makes.
2 The company has an historical association with the product that gives the activity an intangible, if not sentimental, value.
3 The benefit to other products of offering a 'comprehensive' range, to avoid the deflection of customers to other sources of supply.
4 A 'dog in the manger' attitude.

However, a company *can* discontinue an activity if it decides to do so. For many professions this is either not possible or highly undesirable, except where a practitioner has limited his work by announced specialisation. In some cases such an announcement is against the rules of professional conduct, as it is deemed to give the individual an unfair advantage over fellow professionals by implying or claiming special skill. Thus many professionals take their work 'as it comes', some younger firms being pleased that it came at all! But in choosing to embrace *all work* normally associated with a profession by the style of, for example, 'solicitor' or 'accountant', and in preventing announcements about specialisation, those professional bodies have numbed the marketing awareness of their members.

It is quite obvious that a single practitioner cannot personally span the range of modern law or accountancy (and most professions) without reference to outside sources of aid. Such a claim is as difficult to believe as a sign outside a small factory claiming to manufacture everything or anything mechanical. Indeed the opinion has been voiced that these restrictions are contrary to the public interest and inhibit innovation and the development of services provided. It could be that the self-interest of the profession in limiting competition has gained a priority above that of the public's best interest. It is an area of currently conflicting opinion and one requiring further thought and clarification. Of importance in this review is the point made earlier, namely the deadening effect that such restrictions have upon strategic thinking about services offered.

It is best here to set aside these restrictions and search for useful analogies or lessons in the world of commerce. This is not to ignore or belittle them but to put them to one side for the moment. What then are the matters to be considered in devising a strategy for the offering of services? The starting point must be the range of professional work commonly understood by the practitioners and the public. From this base the firm may seek to influence its direction of growth. Narrowing one's focus to that of an existing practice, the review would begin with an evaluation of its existing activities in terms of:

1 The clients' valuation of and reactions to the service.
2 The cost, sales and profitability of each activity.
3 The range of the services provided.
4 The probable future and potential volume of each service.
5 The efficiency with which the service is provided.
6 The quality of the service.
7 The rating of competitors under items 1-6.
8 The areas of under-utilised capacity.

A client's evaluation of a professional service provided by a local firm is not an easy matter to discover. Unlike the rating of a pickle, which is an impersonal matter easily made the subject of street questionnaires, the subject requires tact. Notwithstanding this difficulty, discreet inquiries can be made to ascertain the standing of the firm and the popular opinion of its strengths and weaknesses. It is also possible to find out its rating in the local league as to size by comparing the numbers employed in the various departments.

Understanding the type of work undertaken is a simple matter of reference to records, and a reasonable accounting system should reveal the profitability of each category, if this is not already done automatically.

Forecasting the future potential volume of work is a more conjectural item. In a large city there may be no limit, beyond the capability of the firm to attract and execute the work, to the rate at which it can expand. In the provincial centre and local town, the potential may be determined by the size of the community. The following should be investigated:

1 Past, existing and planned population. These figures can be ascertained from planning offices and seen in future residential land allocations.

2 Anticipated employment. The planned floor area of proposed offices and shopping centres indicate the extent of future development.

3 Proposals for the construction or extension of schools, hospitals and other institutions help to fill in the detail of the picture of the future.

4 Regional development plans are material to the extent that the area under consideration is influenced by regional prosperity, traditional and new industries and improvements in communications. The construction of a new motorway leading to major office and shopping developments can dramatically change the potential of a town in a few years, especially if industrial and residential estates are developed around it.

These inquiries should result in a fairly accurate assessment of the volume of potential business and the type and quality of work that it will generate. Each profession must judge for itself the influences of these changes and the share that it is likely to obtain. Most professions will enjoy certain freedom in influencing their rate of development if they can identify the opportunities in this scene. This is best illustrated by a simple example.

Look at a typical firm of accountants established for, say, fifteen years. The bulk of its business has developed in auditing the accounts of small and medium-sized local retailers. The partners belong to social clubs used predominantly by their clients and they are well respected in the community. Recent years have seen changes:

1 A number of well-established private retail shops have closed upon the retirement of their proprietors, and several have been closed because of the sale of the premises for redevelopment.
2 There is a growing resistance to increasing fees among the smaller retailers who are having difficulty competing with new, larger chain stores and supermarkets. Costs have increased at a faster rate than fee income, and profitability has levelled off though gross fees have increased.
3 The population of the town has expanded considerably by the construction of several large housing estates. However, these are mainly inhabited by breadwinners who commute to a nearby city using the new motorway. The proportion of the population needing advice on personal taxation seems to be declining as the older people retire and fewer people have private incomes.
4 The amalgamation of two leading banks has now resulted in the closure of one branch and the expansion of another. The manager of the closed branch, who used to recommend a steady stream of clients, has gone away and the new manager is a stranger to the area.
5 The firm, on making discreet inquiries, finds that it has slipped from third to ıourth place in terms of people employed.
6 A new industrial estate has been developed on the outskirts of the town comprising several major companies and a range of small manufacturers and service industries. Further units are to be constructed.

In common with many towns the community has undergone a fundamental change. Many people complain that it has lost its old atmosphere and dislike the new office blocks and multi-storey car parks. The total population has increased and so too has the total volume of accounting work. But the pattern has altered. The small shops have diminished and employment has shifted to the industrial areas. The once secure base of servicing the retail trade is diminishing. The centres of influence, once the local businessman's club, have grown smaller in stature. In these circumstances there must be a basic shift in the firm's strategy and attitude or it will lose further ground. Supposing the following courses are examined and adopted:

1 To widen the range of capability and to place more emphasis on auditing and financial services for industry in order, within the code of professional conduct, to be more aware of and attractive to the needs of local industry.
2 To enlarge the geographical area of coverage. The town is well served by communications. Redevelopment has eased access for visitors.
3 To develop and emphasise a taxation and advisory service for the smaller manufacturers, including a small research programme into their present and future accounting systems and needs.
4 To extend the capability for handling more complex problems by linking with a London-based specialist consultancy service and additional staff training.

This example, hopefully not oversimplified, illustrates the way in which, within the constraints of a defined service, a firm can react and create a new strategy for the future. Furthermore, such a plan opens up greater opportunities for future expansion than existed in the previously static market town community. The next, and by no means the easiest, phase is to translate these plans into reality. A number of internal changes are inevitable and may include the following:

a Further training of one or more of the partners to improve rapidly a grasp of the accounting problems of industry.
b Replacement of a senior assistant with a person of proven ability and experience in the industrial field.
c Expenditure of time and money on research.
d Internal retraining and reorganisation to increase speed of service.
e The development of the consultancy and advisory function.
f Conscious and physical effort to attract new work.

The biggest obstacle to such a programme of change may

prove to be the entrenched attitude formed by years associated with small-scale retail trades. Past customers in retailing had required a routine audit of a comparatively simple and repetitive business compared with the more complex activities of manufacture and subcontract work. Many of the retailers were cautious in spending money on professional fees and some even resentful of initiative shown by their advisers. In contrast many of the manufacturers may expect their accountants to tell them of new developments and to contribute more frequently and voluntarily to their management decisions. In conversation among themselves, industrialists often complain that their professional advisers only answer questions instead of thinking of them, that they lack enterprise and seem blithely unaware of the real pressures of highly competitive situations. A mere change of outward appearance will not meet the new demand; a new 'image' will fail unless it is based on a real transmutation of the firm — the root and fibre has to adapt as well as the foliage. The 'new' firm has both to recognise and feel its new role as the provider of a needed service to industry in substitution for its old role of necessary and not highly valued auditors to tradesmen. The firm's view must look forward, constantly searching legislation and situations for constructive advice for the clients. The questions often asked must be rephrased from 'Why should we?' to 'Why shouldn't we?' and from 'Why?' to 'Why not?' In short, the traditional inhibitions have to be recognised for the restraints they often are.

Before turning to the planning and execution of a new policy, one aspect remains and that is its organisation and control. Recognition of a problem will not solve it, and undertaking to do something about it will do little more. A committee or preferably an individual in the smaller firm must be personally responsible for the subject of service strategy and accountable for its progress. In the large firm it may be a full-time task, and the person carrying out the work must be free from other day-to-day responsibilities that might slow the work down. In a small firm the person responsible must be allocated sufficient time to do the work properly. It is essential that there should be no bias. If a specialised person is nominated, then care is necessary to avoid any bias towards his past department or function. The work must be representative of the whole firm and all talents within it. For the purpose of this discussion the person will be called the Services Marketing Manager, which title admits assistants that may have full or part-time responsibilities for different departments. It demands someone who is genuinely interested in the subject and enthusiastic about it, for it involves responsibility for research, creative business thinking, the objective scrutiny and assessment of ideas coming forward, methodical record keeping and control of adopted plans. Above all this person must be orientated to the client and potential client. His performance will be judged on business creation rather than business execution . The Services Marketing Manager will, of course, report to the partnership, board or planning group which ultimately and correctly ensures harmony with the firm's overall objectives.

Setting the stage for the marketing of services

It is difficult to examine the past and present performance of a business without thinking about the future. But there are some further points that need attention. It is one thing to identify a new set of aims for a firm; it is another to achieve them. The principal resource of a professional firm is the skills of its members. The possible need for re-training has already been touched upon, as has the fact that adoption of a marketing philosophy may only be possible after substantial changes in attitude. These changes can prove much easier to talk about than to achieve. It is proable that some staff changes will be necessary. For this reason both job descriptions and the specifications of those who fill them will need modification, and the work of personnel recruitment, selection and development must be completely integrated into the marketing process. The acquisition of certain key people may form stepping stones in the programme. This is particularly the case where the intention is to create *new* business rather than to develop existing activities.

Physical resources are usually of less importance to a labour-intensive practice. Premises and equipment must be judged for their suitability in the future. Professions do not traditionally pay too much attention to their surroundings, and while 'prestige' may not be as relevant to them as to the commercial enterprise, they contribute to the impression created. They must be looked at afresh through the eyes of the clients. In creating a clear identity it is essential that decor, furnishing and location are not ignored. People are partly judged by their surroundings. One cannot expect to project efficiency from a dingy lair on the fourth floor of a back street. Convenient car parking can influence people more than they would often admit when deciding upon whom to consult in congested cities. Taste and moderation are the keywords. Equipment must equally match the planned standards. If the marketing plan expresses an intention to move 'up market', the latest equipment may be essential. For example, in dentistry who boasts about a dentist with a slow drill? Where waiting-room facilities are provided they present a useful opportunity for some professions to exhibit samples of their work, e.g. architects and engineers, by tastefully framed pictures. In some cases literature about the firm or its history may be acceptable, or if this is not considered to be the case, then literature about the profession and its history should be used. The impression, the sometimes vital first impression, is created from the moment that the client enters the building, if not on the telephone when he makes the appointment.

Selling professional services

The traditional view of most professions, particularly the consultative ones, has been opposed to the concept of marketing and antagonistic to selling activity. Strict rules of conduct have been framed that expressly forbid members taking any action that might be interpreted as the solicitation of instructions and price competition is not allowed. Such emotive words as 'touting' and 'canvassing' underline the abhorrence felt of such behaviour by those that conceive it to be 'unprofessional'. To many individuals and their professional bodies, professional dignity is incompatible with advertising or any public announcement beyond a brass plate on the front door. Unprofessional behaviour, that is to say, conduct that could, in the opinion of the governing council, prejudice a member's professional status or the reputation of the Institution or Society, has not been the subject of notable controversy or public feeling. For that matter, rules against supplanting other members of the profession have not been discussed. The main controversies have been about the fixing of fees, advertising, and, to an extent, claims of specialisation. In the conclusion of *A Report on the Supply of Certain Services by Estate Agents, 1969*, the Monopolies Commission stated (subject to a note of dissent of one member), 'We are not impressed by any arguments advanced by the estate agents' committee in favour of estate agents' fees continuing to be charged at standard rates.' And it preceded its final recommendations with the words: 'In order to remedy the mischiefs which result from these conditions. . . '. Since that time additional professions have been investigated, and the general conclusions have largely followed along similar lines. The view of society, in so far as it finds expression in the Monopolies Commission and the decisions of Parliament, seems firmly set against the almost hallowed view of the professional minority, who purport that these restrictions are for the general good. The progressive removal of protective rules of conduct in the growing sector of society that provides services signals that the time is ripe, if not already past, when new and acceptable values must be found — values that preserve professional status, stimulate dignified competition, encourage innovation, provide opportunities for the imaginative, reward the hardworking and profit all. These are attainable objectives well within the grasp of those that approach the subject without prejudice. Each profession is unique and should ideally form its own mould rather than suffer the often crude and badly aimed hammer blows of legislation. As it is quite impossible in a work of this general nature to allow for the nuances appropriate to each discipline, the subject of selling will be treated broadly. It is for each to find his own position of comfort in the tension existing between his rules of professional conduct, the law, contemporary society and his own desire to survive.

> 'The use of the word "technique" when applied to selling frequently engenders a variety of negative reactions. The uninitiated consumer imagines a low cunning to relieve him of his money in exchange for goods that he doesn't want. The professional looks down his nose with disdain. The British, in particular, harbour an innate shyness of salesmen and when the word "technique" is used, which hints of some method of gaining an unfair advantage, the response is immediately to oppose whatever is about to be said.'*

In fact the sales process is a logical sequence of steps, largely of common sense steps, designed to generate the maximum amount of business in a given amount of selling time and cost. The work should be aimed to sell to the right people, that is to say, to those who will be satisfied with the services that they purchase. If the firm's strategy has been correct and the services it offers are well chosen and of good quality, the sale is a process of introduction rather than persuasion. The client's selection of a particular professional adviser should similarly be a sound business decision. The four main steps to be considered are:

1 Prospecting.
2 Explanation or demonstration.
3 Negotiations to adjust the service to the client's needs or to overcome objections.
4 The closing, that is, the final 'taking of instructions'.

Prospecting The task in this phase is firstly to identify and then to assess the prospective client. The market research work will have identified the type of client and work for which the firm is best suited. Thus each partner, executive or assistant coming into contact with the outside world should have a good idea of the profile of the clients that the firm most wishes to cultivate. Where the code of conduct permits announcements in the press or in journals, this will indicate the suitable wording. Where the rules of conduct permit the announcement of a specialisation or the presence of a specialised department,

*M. Allsopp, *Survival in Business*, Business Books.

the matter is greatly simplified for both the practitioner and the potential client. Where the rules or the firm's own policy do not permit announcements or active steps to be taken, the starting place must be the firm's existing clients and professional contacts.

Existing clients are the best base from which to expand any practice and in many cases the most economical. But it is only a fruitful base from which to work if each member of the firm realises that he has a personal responsibility to 'sell' the firm by his standard of personal conduct and quality of work and is trained and motivated to identify opportunities. One of the most unfortunate and common misunderstandings of young professional people is the belief that *non-selling* or *anti-selling* sets them apart from or above those 'in trade'; in fact it probably indicates that they do not possess the qualities necessary for partnership and will reach their ceiling as qualified assistants or employees. It is a sort of misplaced conceit. In terms of prospecting for further business, it also means that each client's affairs must be as completely understood and examined for opportunities as the relationship permits. The following examples serve to illustrate the point:

1 An estate agent selling a house for a company director or company secretary must be keenly aware of the fact that his client may have a need for acquiring or disposing of commercial property for his business. Conversation may reveal an intention to extend a factory of discontentment with a rating assessment. A talk ranging over the subject of property may produce all manner of assignments from the provision of evidence in boundary disputes or litigation with builders to the management of development projects.

2 An architect, retained to design a private house, may find that his client can avoid the cost of moving to larger business premises by modernising the layout of existing facilities. He may lose one job and gain a client for life.

3 A solicitor retained to act in a matrimonial matter may find that his client also has need for advice upon his service contract with his employer or in the matter of his will or in the sale of the matrimonial home and acquisition of future accommodation.

These three examples are sufficient to illustrate several important points about prospecting among existing clients:

1 A client often does not realise the full implications of a problem or need when taking professional advice. Experience is necessary to see most problems in context, and an accurate prognosis will often enlarge a brief, for the benefit of both the client and the professional. This is as much an act of selling as of professional competence, and business comes from the fertility of the practitioner's own mind.
2 The relationship between a client and a professional adviser often has boundaries far beyond the subject matter of the first consultation. The layman, quite understandably, does not always appreciate the range of services available to him. It is up to the professional to explore the circumstances; only he has the knowledge to see where his training can be helpful. Prospecting among existing clients is often a process involving their education as much as inquiry to identify opportunities.

The best method of prospecting beyond the circle of existing clients is obviously by recommendation. There is no better basis for the start of a professional relationship. It must be realised that some clients are better placed to recommend business than others. The private individual, without business involvement, may not be able to introduce more than an occassional friend. On the other hand a bank manager comes across innumerable opportunities to refer customers to accountants, as does a solicitor. Similarly an accountant can reciprocate by recommending his clients to the solicitors or banks that he considers best for his client's purposes. Thus in matters of recommendation it is frequently the case that other *non-competing* professionals are in a position to generate more business than individual clients. Accepting that the cost of professional time is high, selling effort or attention must naturally be directed at these centres of influence to produce the best results. Another constraint in selling is the limitation of available time to meet new people and make new contacts. The following guidelines suggest themselves:

1 The larger the number of people a professional person can

meet, the more likely he is to encounter people in need of his services.

2 Those who hold influential positions, usually but not invariably in related activities, justify an investment of more time than those who are not so placed. The ambitious professional should therefore ensure that such people are aware of:

a The full range of services that the firm provides.

b The areas in which it is particularly skilled or anxious to expand.

c *c* The geographical area over which it is able to under take work.

d Any achievements of particular distinction, e.g. the design of notable buildings or contributions to research of innovation in service.

e The capacity of the firm in terms of staff.

f Its length of establishment or experience of its partners.

g Any notable non-professional activities in sport or culture that give interest to the partners or staff *as people*.

In short he must be aware of the *benefits* that the firm has to offer its clients in terms that the clients understand and can relate to their needs.

Being established in a community really means being known and respected. Some young practitioners make the mistake of spending too much time among members of their own profession. Every qualified person has a duty to support his local branch of the professional body to which he belongs, but for many this environment is the least likely source of work. In terms of selling, it is often totally unproductive. However, there are opportunities for meeting members of other professions and industry through the social and educational functions organised jointly with other organisations, and these have the additional benefit of reminding the professional of the environment and problems of other people as well as being instructive.

Sometimes occasions arise which assist by unsolicited and legitimate publicity. The architectural competition has served to put many young firms on the road to better things. Some legal cases have done much to make the reputation of the lawyers concerned. The first heart transplant made one surgeon internationally famous overnight. One London firm of accountants has achieved eminence in dealing with insolvencies, and a firm of London architects became well known to the man in the street through designs that flowed from its drawing boards during the property boom. At a more local level, opportunities undoubtedly occur for many to advance the interests of their firms, especially those that may be involved in the regular controversies that revolve around new roads, planned developments, the closure or development of schools and hospitals and other public facilities. Local government needs the professional knowledge that a practitioner brings to a debate, and where there is the talent, such activities can quickly make a reputation.

There are ample opportunities available for most professional people to increase their contacts in the society within which they operate, and to direct their efforts towards those people, organisations, societies and places that have the highest probability of furthering their professional interests. One final advantage merits inclusion and that is that one's wife or husband can often be involved, thereby obtaining the satisfaction of making a contribution to what otherwise might be a closed world of which he or she can become resentful.

Explanation and demonstration Most professional bodies have rules that prescribe procedures that must be adhered to if a member is consulted where there is an existing adviser. In such cases reference should be made to those rules. It will be assumed here that the potential client is free to instruct whom he pleases and that the practitioner is free to accept. The objective in the next phase is to show the potential client that:

1 The firm is able to fulfil the proposed demands in terms of skill, capacity, continuity and efficiency.
2 That the commercial arrangements are sensible; this by no means implies that they are the cheapest, but that they offer the best available *value* for the client and are services from which he will benefit.

This phase is less likely to occur in the simple routine operations that form the bulk of work for the small firm. If a man has a toothache he asks around his friends who is the best dentist, by which he often means the nicest or least painful, and he goes along and is dealt with. At the other extreme a well managed company will select its advisers with the same, if not greater, care that it will select its employees. Many firms assume, to their cost, that their ability will be taken for granted, which is quite wrong. The person responsible for handling prospects should be trained, and his presentation should be carefully prepared and immaculately presented. The following is the general procedure:

1 *Research* The potential client's particular needs must be explored. The quality, experience and personalities of the personnel with whom the firm will be liasing must be assessed if possible. It is not uncommon for negotiations to go well at senior level and then to deteriorate after delegation to the routine level of contact. The requisite skills to discharge the work must be assessed, as must the work load that will be generated. The client's stated brief must be scrutinised to ensure that it is a realistic one and that it will permit efficient execution. Areas where the firm, by virtue of its organisation or specialisation, can make a particularly strong contribution will be of special interest as they constitute highly saleable and perhaps unique benefits to the potential client.

2 *Examining the firm's capacity* Once a clear picture of the requirement has been established, it will be possible to plan the firm's capacity in terms of manpower, equipment, facilities and capital. Where personnel would be on semi-permanent detachment to the client, their suitability must be reviewed. The system for communication between the client and the firm must be considered to avoid confused instructions or vague reporting.

3 *Presentation* At this stage the firm presents to the potential client its proposals for carrying out the assignment. It may consist of a written quotation or extend to a lengthy report, proposals and a quotation. It may consist of a semi-formal meeting or a full-scale conference with visual aids. The scale of the operation does not change the nature of it, which is to convince the client that he or his company will make the best choice in selecting the firm.

The client will be watchful for the accuracy with which the potential adviser has grasped his real needs, and careful to observe the approach to their solution. He will be more impressed by proposed contributions than past achievements for other clients, though these may be important. The decision-maker will be anxious to avoid an error, because the consequences of poor professional advice may far outweigh considerations of the cost of fees. Furthermore the envisaged association may extend over a long period and be difficult to sever.

Negotiations It is quite common for the review that occurs in the minds of both parties during these activities to generate new ideas or focus attention on misunderstandings on either side. Flexibility is the keyword, providing it does not lead to an unworkable distortion of the brief. One inevitably meets clients who are excessively self-opinionated, irresolute, muddled, shifty or unlikeable to an extent that dooms the chance of a successful relationship before it starts. In such a case it is better to withdraw, for ultimately the success of the assignment is more important to the integrity of the professional than anything else.

Closing Many people who sell experience the greatest difficulty in bringing their prospect to a point of decision. In many professional matters the contract is finally forged by correspondence, and this provides an opportunity for the good letter writer and communicator to clarify and settle proposals, which can accelerate the closing of an agreement. The final contract probably forms the basis of an agreement lasting for many years. If badly drawn, it may contain the seeds of a future disagreement that could terminate the business. Great care should be brought to the matter to avoid the carelessless that sometimes attends the euphoria following receipt of major instructions.

Summary

As the economic and social environment changes, so must

the professions, by innovation to meet clients' needs with services of the best fit. While tradition may buttress professional ethics against a pressure to reduce standards, it cannot be a substitute for progress. This essential advance must utilise every beneficial concept of modern management that touches upon the development of people, the design of organisations, the planning and control of work, the utilisation of resources and, by no means least, the marketing and sale of skills. An inadequate response can only lead to a reduction in the calibre of practitioners as the talented move into industry and commerce, where rewards will be higher in terms of income, facilities and satisfaction.

Checklist – Chapter 10

MARKETING AND SELLING PROFESSIONAL SERVICES

For the profession as a whole

1 What is the current understanding and attitude towards *(a)* marketing and *(b)* selling as expressed by rules of conduct?
2 What official views have been expressed to *(a)* government and *(b)* members in evidence to government inquiries and explanation of the rules of conduct?
3 Does the professional body maintain a systematic research programme on public needs, market trends, the size of the market and future potential?
4 Does the professional body have a committee or officer responsible for reviewing present and future services, and does that committee have adequate information?
5 How does work traditionally come to the practitioners within the profession?
6 What does the professional body publish for the education and guidance of the public?
7 Is marketing included in the syllabus for the qualifying examinations?
8 How are fees calculated, and what rules bind members to levels of charges?
9 How are fees set and reviewed?
10 Do fees provide reasonable profits on all the services provided?
11 How responsive is the fee system to changes in costs, supply and demand? What influence does government have on prices?

12 What rules govern advertising or announcements of specialisation?
13 What rules govern solicitation and surplanting?
14 To what extent is the profession protected by limitation of entry?
15 How widely available are the services?
16 Are the services conveniently located?
17 What information flows from member firms to the governing body on the market place and client needs?
18 Is marketing included in annual and local conferences?
19 What consultations are held with consumer associations?
20 Are complaints screened for defects in the marketing function?
21 How does the profession compare, in marketing terms, with similar professions abroad?

For an individual firm

1 Do the partners have a proper appreciation of the marketing and sales functions; is the subject discussed formally and are objectives agreed and recorded?
2 Is the firm primarily orientated to its discipline or to its client's needs? Is the marketing passive, responsive or aggressive?
3 Has the firm defined its existing and potential clients in terms of *(a)* their identity, *(b)* their location, *(c)* their characteristics, *(d)* their circumstances that trigger consultation, *(e)* their present and future needs, *(f)* image of the firm and profession in the eyes of the clients, *(g)* any unidentified needs, *(h)* any unused services.
4 Has the firm examined its range of services and its strengths and weaknesses in each area?

5 Is the future development of the community understood in terms of growth and changes of character?

6 How will the firm respond to changes in the market place? Has it a positive marketing plan?

7 How is the responsibility for marketing allocated; to whom and how frequently does that person report? Is adequate time allowed for carrying out the work? Is his brief clear and in writing? Has the person received any formal training in marketing?

8 Do the firm's records reveal the proportion of business in each area? The trend, profitability and percentage growth in each area?

9 Has the firm analysed its competitors, their strengths and weaknesses and trends in their development?

10 Do all staff that can contribute to the marketing and sales policy have a full understanding of it?

11 Has the sales process of prospecting been studied and planned?

12 Have the 'centres of influence', i.e. those people best able to recommend work to the firm, been identified?

13 Does the firm maintain regular contact with important organisations other than its own professional body?

14 What partners are responsible for dealing with prospects?

15 Is the firm able to analyse each prospect and make a sound presentation of its services when required to do so?

16 Are existing clients kept fully informed of the firm's new or developing services?

17 Are the full and complete needs of all existing clients known and serviced?

18 Is sales effort properly directed to the areas required?

19 Does the location and accommodation suit the plans and properly project the firm?
20 Are the furnishings, fittings, equipment and other resources adequate for the present and future demands?
21 Is the pricing of the firm's services competitive, and do costs represent value to the clients?
22 For what reasons are clients lost?
23 Does marketing awareness permeate through-throughout the firm, or is it restricted to senior management?

The powerful cause change,
The foresighted anticipate it,
The clever profit by it, and
The inadequate are engulfed by it.

Survival, **M. Allsopp**

CHAPTER 11

Conclusion — looking to the future

Many of the principles, indeed traditions, of the professions are currently being challenged by economic, social and technological change. The processes of qualification, recognition and establishment no longer assure those who practice the relative security that they might have enjoyed in past years. While the true professional may always be distinguished by the fact that he places his clients' interests above his own, and belongs to a body of people whose common interest is the development of their vocation, these tests are under increasing pressures. The legislature has shown itself to be increasingly reluctant to grant or perpetuate privilege and consequently, for good or ill, the efficiency with which the professions operate is of growing importance to their prosperity and development. Add to this the increasing cost of employing highly skilled people, the competition for their services from overseas, government and industrial employers, and it must be recognised that many practitioners are now in the main stream of business. While the foundation of their reward may be professional skill, their prosperity will increasingly be determined by the standard of their management.

However, management is not a subject that can be picked up and used at will, though it does offer many techniques that can be used in that way. To be of real value such processes as policy formulation, planning, organisation, personnel selection and administration, and financial control must be integrated with daily professional activity and thought. This should start in training and continue until the day of retirement.

Another important benefit that flows from the adoption of a 'management' approach is greatly increased flexibility. The days when a person can spend an entire career in an occupation without witnessing considerable change are over. Not only will the content of some occupations change, some will disappear and new ones will emerge. Flexibility, a keyword in management, is of growing importance.

The professional bodies have a role of ever-increasing importance. In a society where power is increasingly held by organised groups, unity can be a prerequisite of survival. The strength of the relationship that exists between each practitioner and his professional body will determine the strength of a profession to a far greater extent than its identity, eminence, age or the wording of its Charter. To the extent that professionalism resists precise definition it is susceptible to criticism from those who judge by price rather than value. Nevertheless it remains a broad and civilising movement of inestimable value. One only has to experience a society that cannot rely on the integrity or skill of its professionals to realise this.

Enlightened leaders who can steer their professions along coherent lines of increasing value to society are the people who will develop the professions of tomorrow. In so doing they will not only influence our lives, but the attitudes and skills of our judiciary, lawyers, doctors, architects, planners, engineers, chemists, brokers and accountants — in fact all those who provide our essential professional skills: and for this they will merit our gratitude.

Appendix

Learned societies and professional bodies

The details in parenthesis after each body give the designatory letters and the total number of members. Because of variations in methods of grading and studentship status, the total number of members is not calculated on a consistent basis and does not afford a true basis for comparison.

Association of Anaesthetists of Great Britain & Ireland
Room 475, Tavistock House South, Tavistock Square, London WC1 9LE
(None, 2,257)

British Dental Association
64 Wimpole Street, London W1M 8AL
(None, 12,000)

British Institute of Management
Management House, Parker Street, London WC2B 5PT
(FBIM, MBIM, AMBIM, 58,900)

Central Association of Agricultural Valuers
Estate Office, New College, Oxford
(CAAV, 1,288)

Chartered Institute of Patent Agents
Staple Inn Buildings, High Holborn, London WC1V 7PZ
(None, 1,819)

Chartered Institution of Building Services
49 Cadogan Square, London SW1X 0JB
(FCIBS, MCIBS, 8,159)

The Chartered Insurance Institute
20 Aldermanbury, London EC2
(FCII, ACII, 50,402)

The Chartered Society of Physiotherapy
14 Bedford Row, London WC1R 4ED
(MCSP, FCSP, DipTP, 22)

The Faculty of Architects and Surveyors
15 St Mary Street, Chippenham, Wiltshire
(FFAS, FFS, AFAS, AFS, LFS, 1,987)

General Optical Council
41 Harley Street, London W1N 2DJ
(None, n/a)

Headmasters' Conference
29 Gordon Square, London WC1H 0PS
(None, 250)

Incorporated Society of Valuers & Auctioneers
3 Cadogan Gate, London SW1X 0AS
(FSVA, ASVA, 5,238)

Institute of Actuaries
Staple Inn Hall, High Holborn, London WC1V 7QV
(FIA, AIA, 3,262)

The Institute of Administrative Accounting and Data Processing
418-422 Strand, London WC2R
(FAAI, AAAI, LAAI, 7,441)

The Institute of Administrative Management
205 High Street, Beckenham, Kent
(FInstAM, AInstAM, MInstAM, 3,900)

The Institute of Arbitrators
75 Canon Street, London EC4N 5BH
(FCAIrb, ACAIrb, 3,900)

The Institute of Bankers
10 Lombard Street, London EC3V 9AS
(FIB, AIB, 111,070)

The Institute of Building,
Englemere, King's Ride, Ascot, Berkshire SL5 8BJ
(FIOB, MIOB, LIOB, TUIOB, 20,135)

The Institute of Chartered Accountants in England & Wales
PO Box 433, Chartered Accountants' Hall, Moorgate Place, London EC2P 2BJ
(ACA, SCA, 67,147)

The Institute of Chartered Secretaries and Administrators
16 Park Crescent, London W1N 4AH
(FICS, AICS, 25,004)

Institution of Electronic and Radio Engineers
99 Gower Street, London WC1
(CEngFIERE, CEngMIERE, TEng(CEI), 8,387)

The Institution of Electrical Engineers
Savoy Place, London WC2R 0BL
(HonF, FIEE, MIEE, AMIEE, 61,857)

Institution of Mechanical Engineers
1 Birdcage Walk, Westminster, London SW1
(FIMechE, MIMechE, Associate IMechE, 53,146)

Institution of Metalurgists
Northway House, High Road, Whetstone, London N20 9LW
(FIM, MIM, 7,865)

Institution of Mining & Metallurgy
44 Portland Place, London W1N 4BR
(None given, 4,311)

The Institution of Municipal Engineers
25 Eccleston Square, London SW1V 1NX
(FIMunE, MIMunE, 9,975)

The Institution of Plant Engineers
138 Buckingham Palace Road, London SW1W 9SG
(FIPlantE, MIPlantE, 6,825)

Institution of Structural Engineers
11 Upper Belgrave Street, London SW1X 8BH
(FIStructE, MIStructE, 1,892)

The Landscape Institute
12 Carlton House Terrace, London SW1Y 5AH
(FLI, ALI, 692)

The Law Society
113 Chancery Lane, London WC2
(None, 31,522)

The Pharmaceutical Society of Great Britain
1 Lambeth High Street, London SE1 7JN
(MPS, FPS, 1,915)

The Royal College of General Practitioners
14 Princes Gate, Hyde Park, London SW7 1PU
(MRCGP, FRCGP, 2,376)

Royal College of Nursing
1A Henrietta Place, London W1M 0AB
(FRCN, 83,824)

Royal College of Obstretricians and Gynaecologists
27 Sussex Place, Regents Park, London NW1 4RG
(FRCOG, MRCOG, 5,844)

Royal College of Physicians of London
11 St Andrews Place, Regents Park, London NW1 4LE
(FRCP, MRCP, LRCP, 6,587)

Royal College of Psychiatrists
17 Belgrave Square, London SW1X 8PG
(MRCPsych, FRCPsych, c.6,180)

The Institute of Chartered Shipbrokers
24 St Mary Axe, London EC3A 8DE
(FICS, AICS, 2,670)

The Institute of Cost and Management Accountants
63 Portland Place, London W1N 4AB
(ACMA, FCMA, 18,000)

The Institute of Directors
116 Pall Mall, London SW1Y 5ED
(FInstD, 30,000)

The Institute of Legal Executives
Ilex House, Barrhill Road, London SW2 4RW
(FInstLEx, 9,673)

Institute of Linguists
24A Highbury Grove, London N5 2EA
(AIL, MIL, FIL, 5,043)

Institute of Management Consultants
23/24 Cromwell Place, London SW7 2LG
(Not disclosed, not disclosed)

Institute of Management Services
1 Cecil Court, London Road, Enfield, Middlesex EN2 6DD
(FMS, MMS, 9,327)

The Institute of Marine Engineers
76 Mark Lane, London EC3R 7JN
(FIMarE, MIMarE, 7,685)

Institute of Neurology
The National Hospital, Queen Square, London WC1N 3BG
(None, n/a)

The Institute of Orthopaedics
234 Great Portland Street, London W1N 6AD
(None, n/a)

Institute of Practitioners in Advertising
44 Belgrave Square, London SW1X 8QS
(MIPA, FIPA, 1,600)

Institute of Personnel Management
Central House, Upper Woburn Place, London WC1H 0HX
(None, 12,314)

Institute of Printing
8 Lonsdale Gardens, Tunbridge Wells, Kent TN1 1NU
(FIOP, AssocIOP, MIOP, GradIOP, 2,100)

The Institute of Public Relations
1 Great James Street, London WC1N 3DA
(FIPR, MIPR, HLM, 340)

The Institute of Quantity Surveyors
98 Gloucester Place, London W1H 4AT
(FIQS, AIQS, 5,703)

Institute of Supervisory Management
22 Bore Street, Lichfield, Staffs WS13 6LP
(FISM, MISM, AMISM, GradISM, 9,323)

The Institute of Taxation
3 Grosvenor Crescent, London SW1X 7EL
(FTII, ATII, 5,857)

The Institution of Chemical Engineers
George E. Davis Building, 165-171 Railway Terrace, Rugby, Warwickshire CV21 3HQ
(HonFIChemE, FIChemE, MIChemE, 5,903)

The Institution of Civil Engineers
Great George Street, London SW1P 3AA
(FICE, MICE, c.30,500)

The Institution of Electrical and Electronics Technician Engineers
2 Savoy Hill, London WC2R 0BS
(FITE, MITE, Associate ITE, Technician Ass. ITE, Graduate ITE, Student ITE, 12,382)

Royal College of Surgeons of England
Lincoln's Inn Fields, London WC2A 3PN
(FRCS, FDSRCS, FFARCS, MRCS, LRCP, LDSRCS, 46,000)

Royal College of Veterinary Surgeons
32 Belgrave Square, London SW1X 8QP
(MRCVS, 448)

Royal Institute of British Architects
66 Portland Place, London W1
(RIBA, 21,235)

The Royal Institute of Chemistry
30 Russell Square, London WC1
(CChemFRIC, CChemMRIC, LRIC, GradRIC, 25,000)

Royal Institute of Public Administration
3 Birdcage Walk, London SW1H 9JJ
(None given, 5,200)

The Royal Institution of Chartered Surveyors
12 Great George Street, Parliament Square, London SW1P 3AD
(FRICS, ARICS, 40,145

Royal Institution of Naval Architects
10 Upper Belgrave Street, London SW1X 8BQ
(FRINA, MRINA, 6,595)

Royal Society of Medicine
1 Wimpole Street, London W1M 8AE
(None, 10,896)

The Royal Society for the Promotion of Health
13 Grosvenor Place, London SW1X 7EN
(FRSH, AMRSH, LMRSH, MRSH, 20,000)

Royal Statistical Society
25 Enford Street, London W1H 2BH
(FSS, 5,000)

Royal Town Planning Institute
26 Portland Place, London W1N 4BE
(FRTPI, MRTPI, LMRTPI/PAMRTPI, 6,700)

Society of Company and Commercial Accountants
11 Portland Road, Birmingham B16 9HW
(FSCA, ASCA, 8,000)

Index